FIRST-TIME
AUTHOR

suggestions, helpful advice, and hard-earned wisdom

from a seasoned writing teacher, author, editor and publisher

to a writer embarking on a first book

by **TIM BROOKES**

ChamplainBooks.com

a division of barnes | macqueen publishing resources

FIRST-TIME AUTHOR

Copyright © 2014 by Tim Brookes

Champlain Books
a division of Barnes | MacQueen Publishing Resources
47 Maple St., Suite 206, Burlington, Vermont 05401
www.ChamplainBooks.com
www.barnesmacqueen.com

Printed in the United States of America
ISBN-13: 978-0-9884523-8-1
First Edition: August 2014
Library of Congress Control Number: 2014938054

Cover design by Martin Simpson
Book design by Martin Simpson & Janina Hartley

The author is alone is solely responsible for the content of this book and bears all responsibility for any claims arising from the publication of the book.

CONTENTS

WHY DOES A FIRST-TIME AUTHOR NEED THIS BOOK?

It may sound odd, but I didn't realize how hard it is to write a book, even for a veteran writer, until I saw someone else struggle with it.

By that time I had written ten books myself, and had certainly struggled with them, but somehow I assumed that my difficulties were just a sign of my own limitations. I didn't understand what a complex task any book is for *anyone* until I watched the struggle from the outside.

I had assigned a book project to a team of three: a newly graduated writing student, a very capable young guy; an experienced magazine journalist with a deep understanding of the subject matter; and, as the lead writer, an entirely capable veteran who had been a longtime newspaper editor and had also written for newspapers, radio, marketing, advertising — the gamut. Or so I thought.

The grad did a pretty good job with the research; the journalist added her understanding; the veteran coordinated their efforts with regular meetings — but the book just didn't seem to get going. In the end, they ground to a halt, with everyone involved feeling unhappy, confused and frustrated.

I was baffled. If these three couldn't write a book, who could? Finally I decided that the basic problem was that all three had experience in *short forms* — poems, articles, radio spots. A long form such as a book (or, I suppose, an opera) was somehow a different beast, one capable of defeating even their collective intelligence and experience.

Since then I've come to think of a book, non-fiction or fiction, as a writer's minefield, an enterprise that poses all kinds of unexpected and hidden challenges.

It's not just the matter of length — it's that every chapter needs to add its own set of ideas, but those ideas need to connect with every other idea in every other chapter, while also leading the reader through an increasingly sophisticated understanding of the subject. Every chapter, even every page, adds its own set of complexities, so the challenge, in terms of difficulty, rises geometrically.

Strangely enough, though, that's not what makes so many writers give up, or at least that's not exactly the problem. What makes a writer give up is emotional: we run into difficulties we don't understand, and therefore we assume we can't cope with them.

That's what this book is for. It's not a template for writing your first book, or for making that book successful in the marketplace. It's a guide to some of the main dangers or difficulties involved in a book project, with suggestions as to what those difficulties reveal about writing, and how to learn from them. A minefield map.

NOTE

At various points during this book, I'm going
to refer to previous books of mine:

Catching My Breath: An Asthmatic Explores His Illness
Times Books/Random House

Signs of Life: A Memoir of Hospice
Times Books/ Random House

A Hell of a Place to Lose a Cow
National Geographic Adventure Press

Behind the Mask: How The World Survived SARS
American Pubic Health Association

Guitar: An American Life
Grove/Atlantic, Inc.

Thirty Percent Chance of Enlightenment
Percentage Possibility Publications

Endangered Alphabets
Percentage Possibility Publications

I'm also going to mention a book produced by the
students of the Champlain College Publishing Initiative:

Pulitzer or Bust

STARTING OUT

SET A SCHEDULE

Nobody can say how long it will take to write a book. As an experienced writer of books, I can look over my array and say that I managed to write one book in four months, but another is still unfinished after 18 years.

So how do you arrange your life around a core activity that is so uncertain?

If you're working with a traditional publisher for your book, you run into this question right away, as it ties in with the issue of contracts. A publisher will want to agree with you on a delivery date for the manuscript. The publisher wants that manuscript in hand sooner rather than later. It's a project they want to make money from, and the sooner they have it, the sooner they start earning income. They also want to make sure you actually deliver a manuscript (believe me, some authors don't!), and giving you an infinitely flexible deadline may seem to them like an invitation for you to never finish the manuscript.

Equally, as a first-time author, you're going to want to please them. You're going to want to demonstrate that you are swift and reliable and you keep your promises. You're somebody that they're going to want to work with again for a second or third book.

On the other hand, every publisher knows that an unreasonable deadline can kill a book before it is born, so it's to nobody's advantage to demand a clean manuscript in three weeks' time. Many publishers see themselves in almost a parental role: they have more experience with books than you, they have a clearer sense of what is possible and how long it will take, but they also want to set clear boundaries for you, the novice.

All in all, then, the publisher's estimate is probably not a bad one, but it's still only part of the conversation. You're the only one who knows what major distractions or commitments are coming up in your life — knee surgery, a daughter getting married, some other work project — and you should definitely bring these up as you two are discussing the delivery date.

If you're planning to self-publish, the same conversation needs to take place, but it needs to take place between you and yourself. In many respects, that's much harder. Your eager self needs to have a voice, but so does your cautious self. You need to do the same assessment of what impediments are coming up, and you need to be aware that neither of your selves has the publisher's experience to tell you how long this project may take.

Here's my suggestion: if you are engaged in a project you've never done before, especially a project of any complexity, you have no idea how long it's going to take you. It's almost certainly going to take you longer than you think. From the very beginning you have to do your best to estimate how much time you can allocate in your life for research and writing, and then add literally 50 percent for the unexpected intrusions and diversions of real life.

That initial estimate, though, is only the first step.

What you need, whether you're working with a publisher or self-publishing, is a clear but flexible timeline.

Let's say you've allowed yourself two years to produce a clean, well-edited manuscript. You've broken it down into eight months for research, eight months for writing and eight months for editing. That's not a bad rule of thumb. As a first-time author, you're likely to place too little importance on research, and you're likely to underestimate how much work needs to go into revision and editing. This allocation of time into three roughly equal phases, then, is a reasonable place to start. It's important, though, to monitor yourself and your work/time habits, right from the get-go. I suggest you carve out a specific amount of time every week — in fact, the same amount of time on the same days every week — to ensure that you respect the act of writing.

It's very, very easy to demote your writing to second or even third place after other demands on your time: family commitments, maintenance around the house, opportunities to make money faster. You can get to the place where you're saying to yourself, "I'll sit down and write as soon as I've done the laundry." Your timeline is what reminds you that you've made this book a priority, and the laundry will have to wait until after the two hours you've set aside for your book.

Even if you keep to your daily schedule, though, you may find yourself falling behind. We'll deal with that in a later chapter, Life Gets in the Way.

One final suggestion: aim to finish ahead of whatever deadline you set yourself. Two reasons: (a) that way you create a buffer space for the unexpected; and (b) that way you buy yourself more time for final revisions. When that day arrives, you don't want to feel as if you're turning in something hasty. You want to feel as if you're turning in something amazing.

DON'T DISQUALIFY YOURSELF

Writing your first book is a little like having your first child. Because you've never done it before, you can't be certain you can do it and therefore you keep thinking you can't do it. So much about it is new, and novelty itself creates uncertainty. If you're having your first child you can be fairly sure how long the process will take, but that's not true with a book; nor can you be fairly sure that if you do nothing, the book will continue to grow inside you. In fact, if the book does stop growing, it's often not at all clear why, or what you need to do to get it going again.

When you're writing your first book, in fact, you can be fairly certain that at some point you're going to be convinced you can't do it.

Everyone has a different reason for disqualifying himself or herself. For some, it has to do with self-exposure: they start being afraid that by sticking their head up above the crowd, they'll be a target for ridicule or envy. A lot of people suffer from what's called the Impostor Syndrome — the fear that they'll be found out and exposed for being *not a real author*, whatever that may be.

Some people can't get a handle on their material and feel overwhelmed almost from the get-go: there's just *too much*. Some feel they don't have enough life experience, others feel they are too old, too out of touch, that they haven't read enough books, that their vocabulary isn't big enough.

I'm not sure if this is going to strike you as a reassurance or not, but here goes: this self-doubt is an occupational hazard. At some point during the writing of each of my first six books, typically within the first four to six weeks, I was convinced I couldn't do it.

My own weakness (and each of you will have doubts of your own) was the voice that said, "You have to know everything." I'd created a fictitious belief in my mind that anyone who wrote a book was not only an expert on that subject but literally knew everything there was to know.

This fear came at me in different ways. In my first book, *Catching My Breath: An Asthmatic Explores His Illness*, I went to work believing that I had to know and understand every possible dimension, every piece of research, every scientific term — even though the whole reason why I was working on the book was because, after having a massive and terrifying attack, I'd discovered that *nobody* understood asthma completely, just as nobody knew what had caused my attack and nobody knew why asthma was on the rise all over the world.

My second book, *Signs of Life: A Memoir of Hospice*, was on hospice and, more broadly, on the nature and experience of dying. This time my uncertainty took a very specific form: I became convinced that I'd never be qualified to write the book unless I had actually watched someone die. In my imagination, that one missing piece would disqualify everything else I brought to my work.

After my third or fourth book I came to believe that these attacks of self-doubt were actually useful warnings — red flags, if you like. While part of me was rushing excitedly into my project, driven by the exuberance that came from having spent two decades wishing I could be a book author and now finally having my chance, another, unconscious part was saying, "Um…" and trying to draw my attention to the fact that if I was planning to take on the entire medical establishment, I'd better know what I was doing.

What I was feeling, then, was not a total collapse of belief in myself — it was a very useful reminder not to take any shortcuts, to write the best book I could possibly. In that light, this anxious feeling was not going to stop me writing; it was going to stop me writing badly.

Eventually I learned to talk myself through these crises in four ways.

The first, chronologically, was by saying to myself, "You can figure this out. You may not know all the answers now, but you don't have to know all the answers now. You just need to know the answers by the time you start writing."

This is a great mantra, as it reduces both the size of the task and the haste at which you've been telling yourself you need to do it. In my case, I allowed myself the time to explore my subject. I vividly remember going into the university library — the only place where I had access to the Medline database — and telling myself that I had two hours, a whole two hours, to look into all these curious and exciting possibilities: a connection between asthma and thunderstorms? Asthma and tooth decay? Asthma and migraines? Individual pieces of research had thrown up these tantalizing possibilities, and I was going to make use of every minute of those two hours trying to find some solid information that would make sense of it all.

The second tactic I learned to use when I was flooded with doubt was to ask myself, "What am I trying to warn myself about?" As soon as I framed the question that way, the anxiety stopped being general and overwhelming and started being specific and even commonsensical.

When I was working on my hospice book, the same kind of thing happened in a different guise. Even though I was doing a great deal of research on hospice, I had never actually seen anyone die. I hadn't even seen a dead body. How, then, could I claim to be writing a book on the nature of dying? I kept imagining some battle-hardened front-line reporter looking at me and sneering, "What do *you* know about death?"

At first, my reaction to this fictitious critic was to confess he was right, and to feel more and more glumly that I shouldn't be writing this book. Eventually, though, I dragged myself out of this bog of self-doubt by deciding that (a) on the one hand, that voice was right, but (b) on the other hand, I could still write the book. I just had to get closer to my subject.

I did this in two ways, one intentional, one certainly not.

When I had been writing the asthma book, I had come to believe I'd never understand asthma until I had actually seen a lung — close up, in real life. So I arranged to observe open-chest surgery, looking over the surgeon's shoulder. I'm still not sure it taught me much about asthma, but it was a fascinating experience.

So this time I put out feelers to see whether I could actually view one of the cadavers used to teach the pathology classes at the local medical school. It turned out to be much easier than being in an operating theater — after all, there's not exactly much risk of my infecting anyone — and extraordinarily illuminating. Apart from anything else, it helped reduce my own fear of death.

As for my sense that I wouldn't really understand hospice until I had seen someone die under hospice care, and had seen how that tender and enlightened process differed so dramatically from the cold, confusing, unexplained, inhumane death my father had suffered in hospital a decade previously — well, I got my wish in a manner I hadn't planned and didn't want: my mother was diagnosed with cancer of the pancreas, and six months later died, my sisters and me standing around her. In doing so, she gave her final gift to her children: she showed us that dying in the right place, under the right circumstances, with the right preparation, was not the terror we imagined.

So in a sense my fictitious hard-nosed reporter had given my a valuable warning. It was my own reaction to the warning — that I should give up on writing the book — that was wrong. Once I had dragged myself beyond that anxiety barrier, everything moved forward, and I never seriously doubted myself again.

The third conclusion I reached after thinking long and hard about this barrier of fear was that it wasn't a barrier at all, except perhaps in the sense of a striped red-and-white barrier that is lowered across a border. I came to think of it as a boundary experience, a sign that I was moving out of the comfort zone I knew well and into unknown territory. Here's the thing: if you're going to write a book worth reading, you'd better move into unknown territory — unknown to the reader, and unknown to you. Without crossing that border, you never bring back anything new for the reader, and you never have the sense of discovery in yourself that animates and drives the act of writing.

The very fact that you're having a hard time finding good information, or a hard time making sense of it, may actually be a sign that you're getting somewhere new. What good would it be to write a book if it took so little effort that anyone could do it? Once I realized this, I added a signature to my emails that stood for several years as my motto: "If it were easy, someone else would already have done it."

These various responses to gnawing self-doubt meant that with each book, writing became a little easier — not technically or mechanically easier, but (perhaps more importantly) emotionally easier.

I didn't come to my fourth realization until I took on an assignment that put me almost completely over my head. I was writing a book, *Guitar: An American Life*, that set out to be the story of the guitar in America and, at the same time, the story of watching a world-class luthier make me a handmade guitar, the two strands weaving together until the end of the book saw the completion of the guitar and the arrival of the guitar's history at the present day.

I was having a great time working on this book. Who wouldn't? I was doing my usual heavy-duty dive into research, tracking every occurrence of the word "guitar" in the *New York Times* from 1851 until the 1960s (and finding utterly wonderful and utterly unexpected stories at every turn). But I was also having a great time savoring the experience of watching wood take shape in a small workshop in birch/spruce/maple woodland in Vermont, the luthier surrounded not only by his tools, glues and oils but also by the very raw materials themselves.

But then I was offered the chance to do a book on the SARS pandemic, a book that would require me to go to Hong Kong, where I'd always wanted to go, and to tackle a subject of genuinely global significance. Here was the catch: I had to do *Behind the Mask: How The World Survived SARS*, start to finish, in sixteen weeks, including visits to Hong Kong, Geneva and Toronto.

I reckoned that I was a little ahead of schedule on the guitar book, which was due in June, and that I could insert the SARS book between late November (in other words, right away) and March. I spent a month going to the library every day reading the *South China News* and the *Straits Times*, *The Economist* and the Toronto papers, and then interspersed my flights abroad with phone interviews to Vietnam, China, Taiwan, the U.K. and probably some other places I've forgotten. By the time I reckoned I was ready to write, and I'd worked out what my table of contents would look like, I had to write a chapter a day.

This may sound like a nightmare, and before I started I fully expected to collapse in a raving, twitching heap, but the time pressure was actually very liberating. The pace at which I had to work meant that I simply couldn't obey my primal conditioning and try to know everything and include everything. All I had time to do was spend the morning telling the story of SARS in Vietnam, or Singapore, or China, and the afternoon and evening checking over my notes, making sure I hadn't forgotten anything really important, and then correcting what I'd written and smoothing out the transitions.

I couldn't possibly know everything, and even if I did, I didn't have the time to tell the reader everything. All I could do was know pretty much what I was talking about, and then tell the story. (And then, of course, send the chapter off to my contacts in each country and beg them to clean up anything important I'd left out or misunderstood.)

Which led me to my fourth realization, or motto: *as an author, your job is to be interesting.* Not omniscient. Not the smartest guy in the room. Not "literary," whatever that means. Just really interesting.

This perspective came in handy right away. As soon as I'd finished the draft of the SARS book and sent it off all over the world to be read and annotated, I had to get back to the guitar book. I started writing the way I had always planned to write it, and the first three chapters ran to about 140 pages. At that rate, I calculated, the book would end up some 1,200 pages long.

Ten years previously, that would probably have driven me to anxiety, insomnia, indigestion, hair loss. Thanks to my experience with the SARS book, though, I thought, "Your job is to be interesting." I went through all my raw materials and pulled out only the stuff that really, really interested me — the bits and pieces I felt were well written, or that I could imagine telling people in a bar. Those pieces alone came to about 350 pages. That was my book.

A lot of factual material (even material that had never been widely published, and that I was pretty sure almost nobody knew) ended up being left out. I wasn't writing an exhaustive academic history: I was writing a book I wanted people to want to read. My job was to be interesting. Everything seemed suddenly very easy. And the book, by the way, was very successful — especially among guitarists, most of whom, I'm pretty sure, tend not to read academic histories 1,200 pages long.

When we set out to write a book, the sheer size of the task, plus the tradition that a book is more intellectually ambitious than a little article/short story/newsletter/essay/review, affects our sense of who we think we are. Our own voice in our own head can start to sound unbearably pretentious, or lame, or glib, or shallow, or idiotic. As soon as that happens, writing can become unbearable. We stop. We dither. We have no idea how to get back in the saddle.

Don't mistake those warnings. They're probably happening for a reason, and maybe even a valuable reason. But they're only warnings. They're not the end of the world or the end of your book. You don't have to know all the answers now. You just need to know the answers by the time you start writing. If it were easy, someone else would already have done it. And in the end, you only have to be interesting.

FEED YOUR HEAD

Remember how I said, at the end of the last chapter, "You just need to know the answers by the time you start writing?" Well, I'm now going to say something that may sound suspiciously like the opposite.

Before you start writing, before you even start writing an outline, before you even start writing notes, you need to face up to a truth most of us try not to admit: *You don't know enough to write this book.*

Or to be more specific (and less discouraging): You don't know enough to write this book *yet*.

Why do these statements not contradict each other? Because it's not yet time to start writing. Not by a long shot. You know all those movies in which the writer starts working on a book by sitting down at the desk and putting a clean sheet of paper in the typewriter? That's not how you start working on a book. And in fact I warned you about this, way back in Chapter 1, when I suggested you think of research, writing, and editing as demanding roughly equal amounts of time.

So here's the truth that a dismayingly large percentage of first time authors try to ignore: I don't care how smart you are or how much you know, and equally I don't care if you're writing non-fiction or fiction. You need to do some research.

I used to hate and dread research. I went to one of the world's greatest universities, which had one of the world's greatest libraries, yet I went into it precisely twice, once to register and once in pursuit of a girl whom I promptly lost in the labyrinthine stacks.

But when it came time to write my asthma book I had no choice but to spend weeks, then months, then ultimately a year and a half researching my subject, and to my amazement it was not only fascinating — it was fun. For the first time in my life, I could hardly wait until the university library opened in the morning. Now research is always my first step in working on a book.

A quick aside here, directed at fiction writers: you, more than anyone, are likely to want to get away with doing less research than you need. Fight that impulse with all your strength.

Every year I read dozens of novels-to-be in which the hero fights the villains, and in every case the author has never been in or seen combat that took place anywhere but on a screen. Every one of them makes me want to pound my forehead against the nearest wall.

Look. Let's dive right into the heart of sword-and-sorcery fantasy. Let's go back into the long series of poems, stories, films and games that make up the King Arthur legends. Let's skip back over Disney and Tennyson and go back to Sir Thomas Malory, who wrote or rewrote or compiled the prose epic entitled *Le Morte d'Arthur* (the death of Arthur), out of which most of the later versions developed.

What makes Malory's narrative so powerful, and even (in its fashion) convincing, is his depictions of combat. Knights get scared. Knights get tired. And at the end of the battle, crows and ravens flock to the battlefield to peck out the eyes of the corpses.

We don't know much for sure about Malory's life, but it seems pretty certain that before becoming a member of Parliament, and before he was imprisoned in the Tower of London (where he wrote

Le Morte d'Arthur to pass the time), he was a professional soldier. He had been on the battlefield, and had probably seen the grisly birds, not to mention the thieves who carried long, thin knives to slide through the knight's visors to make sure they were dead before robbing their corpses.

You may not have that experience, but you can certainly make a worthwhile effort to research your novel, by reading or by interviewing people who can give you first-hand accounts.

So. Fiction-writer or non-fiction-writer, you need to do an awful lot of research before you start writing. It'll give your writing more credibility, and it will also make your ideas, your darling children, more subtle, nuanced, textured.

The last thing I want to say on the subject is a self-correction: it's not an awful lot of research. It's a wonderful lot of research. When I was researching every one of my books, I came across material I had no idea existed and was often so fascinating/surprising/important I couldn't possibly have made it up. Research not only makes you a better writer, it makes you a better person. Try it.

WRITER'S BLOCK?
NO SUCH THING

There is no such thing as writer's block.

Before I get flamed by a hundred thousand writers who have spent far too many hours staring at a blank sheet of paper or a blank screen, getting steadily more anxious, depressed and/or frustrated, let me clarify what I mean: there are many ways to get stuck as a writer, but to call any of them writer's block doesn't help. It is at best a misunderstanding of the way writing happens and at worst a way to sabotage yourself.

Or to put it another way: Writer's block? It's all in your head. (This pun was coined by Becky Schmidt, a former student in the Professional Writing Program at Champlain College. It is now on the ballpoint pens we give away to students when they graduate from the program.)

I'm not saying that writing always comes easily to me and if it doesn't come easily to you, there's something wrong with you. Every writer runs into all kinds of obstacles — and that's exactly the point I'm making. Writing consists of a considerable number of different activities, and different problems can derail you at different stages in the writing process. The reason why I'm against the phrase "writer's block" is that it doesn't help you figure out what's holding you up, or what to do about it.

Let's take just a few of the conditions that can stop you from writing.

The classic Hollywood illustration of writer's block is the writer who just can't get started. He (for some reason, writers in TV shows and on the big screen are usually guys) is ready to write, sitting at the keyboard, but either no ideas come or he writes a series of first lines that get stupider with each passing hour, and the pile of balled-up sheets of paper in (around, nowhere near) the wastepaper-basket rises to knee height, thigh height, hip height, and so on.

That's not writer's block — that's a writer who is under the delusion that you just sit down and start writing at page one. As this book makes clear, I don't believe that's the best way to start writing, and in fact I don't know any practicing writer who starts that way. The good idea comes in the car, in the shower, in conversation, while reading the paper — and it gets nursed and nourished in your head for days, weeks, even years before you're ready to start writing.

Granted, that process can be really, really frustrating and anxiety-provoking, especially if your income and your family are depending on it. I have stayed up way too late on many a night beating my brains trying to come up with a good idea for a magazine article or a book, but that's not writer's block. It's just impatience and a refusal to accept that good ideas don't come when called. And even when they come, the worst thing you can do is sit right down and try to start at page one. As Bob Dylan wrote, "I'm going to know my song well before I start singing." The best thing you can do is to get to know that idea well before you go anywhere near a keyboard.

Yes, you'll still be faced with strategic choices about where to start, but those are not panic-driven. Try one starting point, then try another. It'll be pretty clear which works best. Decisions to be made, but no block.

Another common panic point is when you've done a whole mess o' research but have no idea how to pull it all together into some kind of orderly beginning-middle-end structure. You may be surrounded by files, or piles of notes; you may have all the data on your computer; you may have gone insane and stuck Post-Its over every wall, window and item of furniture. You have no idea where to start writing and, to make matters worse, you may try to avoid your dilemma by doing yet more research.

Again, this is not the dreaded writer's block — it's a failure to understand how research and thinking and writing come together.

In truth, you're probably being bedeviled by a hobgoblin who has been lurking in your mind since college, or even high school, a hobgoblin who says that research and writing are two different things, and you do one, then you do the other. That hobgoblin sequence misrepresents the way our minds work.

As soon as we unearth a new piece of information, our minds instinctively go to work on it, trying to connect it to other data, trying to find or make patterns. If we're smart, we'll not only let our minds do this, we'll encourage them to do so, and we'll document the process, by keeping some kind of writer's journal or at least by making note-taking an active process that includes our own reflections and commentary on what we've just discovered. It's like making notes in the margins of the mind. And those notes can easily aggregate to the point where we're writing sentences and even paragraphs, research flowing instinctively into writing.

Again, you'll still be faced with strategic choices about where to start, but again those are not panic-driven, nor do they need to be panic-inducing. That's what writing is all about: you get to make up the rules, but you have to make the choices. It's what you signed up for.

The third common blockage-point happens midway during the actual writing process. You're working your way through your plot or your outline or your table of contents, when it gradually dawns on you that the damn thing will not fit together. You have A–M, and you have plans for N–Z, but you can't see how the hell you're going to get from M to N.

Again, this is not some dreaded psychological block. This is simply an error in structure. Or to be more exact, you've chosen form over content, and the content simply won't fit the form. Your outline or plan no longer works because life (in this case the life of the mind) has got in the way. Your own thinking has steadily outgrown the small box you gave it at the beginning, and when you can't force it back in its box, you think it's because you can't write.

The truth is, you *can* write — in fact, you can write more interestingly and more expansively than you expected to. Instead of writing a convoluted and unconvincing rope bridge from M to N, you need to step back and look at the new subject, the new material, and give it a new shape. That's not easy, but it's very good for you, and it's essential for your growth as a writer.

That leads neatly to the next point: *difficulties are signs of growth, or at least the opportunities for growth.*

I didn't realize this myself until I was teaching a wonderful three-hour weekly evening class made up of both traditional and non-traditional students. I walked in some time early in the semester and several people immediately started telling me about difficulties they had run into in trying to do that week's assignment. Luckily, I was just smart enough to realize that this was a sign that the students were setting the lesson plan: they were telling me what they needed to learn right now, regardless of what I had planned to talk about that class.

It also occurred to me that by identifying their difficulties, they were telling me what they needed to learn as writers. If they didn't encounter problems, they weren't breaking any new ground. Every difficulty, in fact, had the potential to lead to *exactly the discovery they needed to make next.*

From then on, I began every class by asking, "What difficulties have you run into since last class? What discoveries have you made?" Those two questions alone would take up the first hour of the class, and the students were as engaged as I could ever have hoped for, because we were working on their agenda and their schedule.

Let's address one last manifestation of that phantom called

writer's block. This is one I come across especially in young or inexperienced writers, and it happens when the writer gets into a very dark place, saying to him- or herself over and over, "I don't like the sound of my own voice/nobody will like what I'm writing/I hate everything I write/I'm not a real writer."

He or she may in fact write fragments, or even whole finished pieces, but then read them over and trash them in fits of frustration and self-hatred.

This obstacle really is psychological, but once again it's based on a misunderstanding about writing.

It goes along with the question I hear often: "Should I write for myself or should I write for my reader?" None of it is a matter of skill; it's all a matter of development. It's all a sign that the writer is moving from being a private individual into a public realm, and their writing is the bridge to that public.

Let me explain. When we first start writing, we write in a sheltered environment where few people see our writing, not much is at stake, and in any case we have very little sense of the broad world. Our parents, with luck, bless us; our teachers, with luck, encourage us. We're in the childhood bubble. We have not learned to be self-conscious, let alone self-critical.

Once we start writing to be read, everything changes. It's like the shower singer going on stage, or the karaoke singer heading into the concert hall: we're self-conscious, we may be hypercritical of our efforts (or, less often, hypocritical), and above all we are starting to learn *what works* — what makes people laugh, what makes them sit up and pay attention, what moves them. We are perfectly capable of learning those skills, but it takes time.

This version of writer's block is tough to overcome, but it's not a sign we can't write or that we're blocked. It's a sign we're learning exactly what we need to learn, and the only way through it is by spreading our radius of readers, asking for responses, listening to or watching their reactions and adjusting accordingly.

As I say, it's a developmental stage. We all go through it. The only danger is to mistake it as a sign of the worst — to call it the dreaded writer's block and, deep down, start panicking. Don't go there, my friend. Put down that gun. Grant yourself a little time, work out exactly what's causing your trouble, and come at it from another angle. You can do it.

THINK LIKE A DOG

The early phases of writing a book are far more about questions than about answers.

Research is not just about gathering facts. It's also about gathering questions.

Every book answers a question, though answering that question also involves answering many smaller questions.

It helps to have a sense of what some of those questions are from the moment you start working. With luck, in fact, it is a question, or a cluster of questions, that has been your incentive to write on this particular topic. But you have to expect that the more you learn, the more that question may be refined or modified. It will also probably lead to other subtler, more penetrating questions.

Let's take a specific example. When Natalia Yaacob and Ian Frisch, students working for CCPI (Champlain College Publishing Initiative) set out to write the book that eventually became *Pulitzer or Bust*, they had a fairly well-defined sense of what the overall question of the book should be: What are the important experiences that help a teenager with an interest in writing become a practicing adult writer?

(Note: This initial overall question is usually conceived by the author or by the author and editor together. It is so central to the whole mission that both parties have to agree on it, and have confidence that it's a worthwhile, interesting question that they will be able to tackle.)

Natalia's and Ian's plan of action was to interview high school seniors and current undergraduates and graduates who were now actively pursuing writing careers, and use those responses as a basis for the book.

This was a good plan. The trouble with this big, overarching question, though, is that people often don't think in big-issue terms, and as such it may be hard to answer those interview questions in a useful way. If I walk up to someone on the street and ask, "What is your philosophy?" or "What are the ten most important encounters you've had in your life?" there's a good chance the person will feel put on the spot and uncomfortable, and there's almost no chance that the answer(s) I get will represent the full depth and richness of what that person might know.

What I suggested to Natalia and Ian, then, was that they ask questions that were more *specific*, and that they ask for *stories*. (You'll notice, of course, that right now I'm answering a question, to a large extent, by telling a story.)

They chewed this over for a while, and came back with a list of interview questions. What was the most difficult challenge you've faced as a writer within the past year? How did you tackle it? What did you learn about yourself, and about writing, from the experience?

Likewise a fiction writer is asking questions all the time. Where would A and B meet? What would they see and hear around them? What would they be thinking and feeling at that moment? How would their conversation begin?

Questions are very interesting creatures. Questions are the means by which we express our curiosity, and as such they are also the forces that suggest our directions of inquiry. They are not only the hinges of the open and inquiring mind; they are the keys that fit and open specific doors, and as such they also generate our sense of direction.

Some people are afraid of questions, because they seem to be a sign of instability. They'd be much happier with an outline, which seems to promise steady progress, a clear sense of direction. Yet an outline can very easily become a cage; it can limit your sense of the scope of the subject, and can thus limit your thinking.

A question is based on what we think we know, and what we think we need to know. Once we ask that question, things change. Questions keep your subject and your mind alive. Asking a question, and getting an answer, changes the questioner, and thus the question.

So put questions to work for you. Make lists of things you don't yet know. Make lists of things you're curious about. Make lists of terms you've come across but don't (yet) understand. Make lists of people you wish you could talk to or books you wish you could read. But don't be intimidated by these lists. They're not must-do lists; they're lists of possible avenues that you can explore if you run dry or want to try a fresh tack.

While we're on the subject, don't be afraid of fresh tacks. You don't have to follow one line of thought doggedly to the bitter end. Allow yourself to move away from one area for the time being to try another. It doesn't mean you're going to dabble forever and never get anything done. It means you're human. All of us get tired of something after a while and need a break from it. Come back to it later and see if your enthusiasm for that avenue of thought has been rejuvenated. If not, go away and come back again after doing something else. Rinse and repeat.

We may discover that the question isn't a very good question, and decide to change the question. We may discover that the question is the wrong question, and decide to change the question. We may think that the question was a good question until we've been given a dozen or a hundred answers, and those answers change our understanding of the situation in such a way that we need to change the question. We may ask a question so penetrating that it reveals a layer of understanding that was completely hidden to us before, so we now need to ask other questions that we couldn't have imagined when we were starting out.

Any or all of these things may happen. It's natural. It's part of the process of exploration. *Asking questions is not simply about getting facts: it's about gathering an understanding.* And what we end up understanding will almost always be larger, more complex and more interesting than we'd dreamed at the outset. What's more, the only way we could have reached that vast, swelling comprehension was by asking questions — in fact, by asking shallow or outright rival questions at first, and gradually seeing where and how to dig a little deeper, and a little deeper.

What all this means is that this process is a wonderful, even mystical thing, but it presents two dangers to the first-time author.

One danger lies in sticking with the initial set of questions and not allowing yourself to accept uncertainty — that is, to accept that as you work on this book, you're going to learn, and change.

If you don't accept that you yourself are part of the process, you're in danger of being like a student taking an introductory course in journalism who goes off to that first interview with a list of twenty questions and is terrified of deviating from that list. The fact is, the best questions are the ones that occur to you as you listen to your subject talk, questions you could never have predicted back in your dorm room the night before when you were making that desperate list of twenty questions.

By the same token, shallow questions get shallow answers. Look at any set of man-on-the-street single-question interviews (sometimes called vox pop, short for *vox populi*, the Latin phrase for "the voice of the people") or single-question surveys, and you'll see that the answers are not only obvious and trivial, but actually raise more questions than they answer. You've got to listen to what people tell you, and think about it. The answer is just the beginning.

The other danger lies in losing your initial sense of purpose.

The more you open up your subject, the more different possible directions open up to you. In any project of this kind it's possible to carry on the inquiry or exploration phase forever. Just as you need to step back every so often and fine-tune your questions, you also need to step back and consider where your questions are taking you.

One way of making sure you don't get lost in your subject is by limiting your time. If you've given yourself three months for this phase, for example, then you want to take a breath every two weeks and ask yourself how you're doing. What are the interesting or promising areas? Where are the gaping holes? What can you realistically achieve in the time remaining? After all, nobody can learn everything, even in an infinite amount of time. Your job is simply to do the best job you can in the time available.

Alternatively, you can limit yourself by area. (This takes more self-discipline.) When your questions take you in a new and unexpected direction, which happens more often than not, you should face down your own curiosity and enthusiasm and ask yourself "Is this a good direction?" Sometimes the new direction will make you throw out half of what you've done so far, and you need to say "No, that's a different book." Seriously. By far the most common source of ideas for your second book will be the material you stumbled on but couldn't use in your first book.

This is just as true of fiction as of non-fiction, by the way. In fact, if your first novel is successful your editor may well want you to write a sequel, so all that extra research and understanding will have a home after all!

The more you find out, the more it modifies what you want to find out. In some respects you may move quite some distance from your starting-point and the questions you were asking at first. That's what has happened to me in at least half the books I've written, and that's entirely okay. It's not a sign you're getting lost: it's a sign you're finding what is really interesting about your subject, not what you once thought was interesting.

Use social networking. Join groups on Facebook or LinkedIn

that consist of people in the area about which you're writing. Throw questions out into the group. Intelligent people like being asked intelligent questions — you'll get a lot of responses, some of which may be very helpful. More people are willing to help you than you could ever imagine.

Don't think like a writer — think like a dog. Trust your sense of smell. Anything that smells remotely interesting, go over and sniff its butt. The point is, you don't yet know the full scale or scope of your subject. You don't know what information is available, or where. You don't even know what you don't know.

If this dog metaphor is getting too graphic and disgusting for you, think of this as the vacuum-cleaner phase. Think of yourself as one of those vacuum cleaners with a headlight, and what you're doing is trundling around vacuuming up anything that you find. (Of course, vacuum cleaners don't have a dog's sense of smell, so this metaphor is not very exact. I include it here only for the squeamish.)

If you think this sounds a lot like hard work (or, heaven help us, *research*), then you've misunderstood why a dog sniffs things. A dog sniffs because it's trying to find things that will interest it.

This is a wonderfully liberating notion. In the past you have probably done pieces of writing that involved research that you didn't choose, or you didn't want to do, and I'm the first to admit that this can be deadly. Now that has changed. Unless you've made the ghastly mistake of proposing a subject just because you thought it could get you a book contract, or just because you thought it would sell a lot of copies, or just because you thought it would be easy (and that really is a ghastly mistake: you might as well just have chosen to spend a year of your life in a dungeon), then those bad old days are behind you.

You are now being paid to be curious, and to be alert, and to sniff around wherever your sense of smell leads you. It doesn't get any better than that. You'll become a more interesting person, a more knowledgeable and engaged person, and at the same time a humbler and a wiser person. Nobody could ask for more.

What sets you free during this phase is the fact that you don't have to make sense of it all yet. You don't have to organize; you don't have to write. You don't have to worry about the number of chapters or the structure — in fact, you can be pretty sure that if you do start thinking about structure or appropriate language or tone or style, you will start worrying.

We'll discuss organization in a later chapter. For the time being, let all that go. You don't need to be that person yet; your job is to be your inner dog. What you discover as the dog will answer all your questions; and conversely, if you try to answer those later-phase questions now, it'll be like putting your inner dog on a muzzle and leash.

This is my favorite phase of writing a book, in many ways, because the possibilities are still infinite. There's no telling what I'll find. And pretty soon — while working on my first book, in fact — I learned that what's out there in the world is infinitely more fascinating and unpredictable than I'd supposed. Or than most people suppose, actually.

Not only can you roam farther than you've ever roamed before — you may, if you work on your book for two years or more, roam farther than anyone has gone before. That's not to say that you'll know more than anyone in the world, but you may well end up having insights that nobody else has ever had, or asking questions that nobody else can answer. That's an extraordinary rush.

CLEAN AND ORGANIZE
YOUR DESKTOP

Having spent an entire chapter telling you that your chief operating principal in this early phase is to follow your nose, and that you shouldn't get caught up in trying to structure or even to make sense of what you find, I'm now going to tell you something that may seem to go in the opposite direction, but is in fact very much the same principle. I'm going to say that from the very start, you need to think about organizing your information.

How am I not contradicting myself? Okay, here goes.

Just as you don't know what your questions will be in two weeks' time, you often don't know which answers will be valuable in two weeks' time. You can't yet know what will connect in an interesting way to something else, or what single fact will turn out to be the gateway to an entirely new field. Yet you need to keep a good record of where you've been, or else you'll simply forget most of what you've discovered. You have to be on top of what you're doing, yet at the same time you have to leave yourself open to serendipity. Here's what I suggest.

Just as you start with a single overarching question, you start with a single repository for what you find out. In the old days that would have been a paper file, or a large cardboard box, or a series of shelves. Nowadays let's call it a single file on your computer (backed up every night, of course) that we can call Research.doc.

Obviously, it doesn't make sense to use just that one file to store all the research you do. It'd be like covering your desk with a million scraps of paper. But the point is, you don't yet know where your nose is going to take you. And as it's now very easy to copy and paste, we can start out with just the one file. Just make sure that you make note of the source of everything you put in that file — title, author and page number if it's a book, URL if it's online — and the name of the person and his/her contact information if it's a personal interview or conversation.

At the moment, then, your organization only consists of two forces. One is selection: you're noting what you find interesting and potentially useful. The other is recording: you're making sure the possibly valuable material doesn't get lost. That's a pretty lightweight and open superstructure. You're not going to break your back or cage your imagination by doing just that.

After a while, you'll start to get a sense that you've found various areas that you're pretty certain you're going to write about. *It doesn't matter that you don't yet know what you'll say or how much you'll write.* All you're doing is replacing the one huge bucket called Research.doc with several smaller and more targeted ones. When I was working on my guitar book, these early categories were pretty obvious: Blues.doc. Rock'n'roll.doc. Classical.doc.

Again, the trick is to allow yourself to think *This is pretty simplistic, but this is all I can do, and all I need to do for now.* If you put too much pressure on yourself at this early stage to know exactly what you're doing, you'll freeze up. Equally, if you're too loose, you'll give yourself a huge mess to deal with. So what you're creating is a *provisional* organizational structure, just as you created a *provisional* list of questions to follow. The two processes go hand in hand.

As it happens, my research into the development of what I thought of as classical guitar made me realize that (a) the phrase "classical guitar" is really a remarkably recent one, and (b) it's not at all useful or accurate. The guitar developed at different times and in different ways in, say, Spain, France and England, and as I started finding interesting stories from each country it made sense to create different files for each. And my reading about France led me to follow the guitar across the Atlantic to the French settlements in North America, and the same thing happened with Spain and England. So France.doc led to another file called New France.doc, Spain.doc led to New Spain.doc, and so on.

This process of addition and subdivision goes on and on. By the time the book was finished I had more than 400 files, some of which were only a few paragraphs long. But the actual number of live or operating files was much smaller: the majority of those 400 files were by then sitting in a directory called Sorted, which meant that the material in them had been taken out and distributed into other, newer files that more closely corresponded to chapters. Jazz.doc, which had become hopelessly big and diffuse, had been broken down into specific periods, plus a new, seminal chapter on New Orleans. Surf.doc had become part of a bigger pre-Beatles chapter. But all the original files were still there in case I changed my mind.

If you're following this closely, you'll notice that I seem to have been creating trouble for myself. Some of these filenames are thematic (Blues.doc) while other are chronological or geographic. Wouldn't this be a nightmare later?

Again, the answer is yes, it would have been if I had stuck too rigidly to the categories. But the keyword is "provisional." These are not chapter headings. These are just increasingly targeted buckets in which to keep my notes.

Just as I suggested that, every two weeks or so, you stop and look over the questions you're asking, the same is true of your files. By and by I decided that the whole story would be roughly chronological, but some of the thematic content also fitted into the timeline. The Hawaiian guitar boom, for example, had its roots in events starting in the early 1820s but really got underway between roughly 1885 and 1915. Likewise, the development of the electric guitar was an important concept and theme, but it also had its place in the timeline. So I could intersperse time-based chapters and topic-based chapters that fitted in among the time-based ones, and *voilà*: I had the basis of an overall structure. I could start moving material from file to file, renaming files and organizing the facts, quotes and thoughts according to this general principle — which hadn't occurred to me until probably six months into the research.

So now let's get really radical. In both the asthma book and the guitar book I found there was a kind of chapterette that kept coming up but didn't fit into the overall organizing structure at all.

Again, the trick is not to panic, not to throw anything out, to keep following your nose and keep writing what seems interesting and at least potentially relevant. Most of the asthma book was a series of inquiries into factors that might explain why asthma is on the increase worldwide, but as I was working on the book, I couldn't help noticing that my own asthma was getting better. So I wrote a series of what might be thought of as journal entries, documenting this developing first-person perspective. In the end, they went into the book: I called them Patient Progress Report I, Patient Progress Report II, and so on. They added a different thread, a different narrative, a greater sense of immediacy, and a more personal perspective. It would have been less of a book without them.

One other suggestion. As soon as you create these well-defined categories or files that you're pretty certain you're going to develop as your table of contents, you start excluding material. While you were still loose and open in your filing, anything could get chucked; now you start discovering more and more odds and ends that don't fit into the structure you've chosen.

This can be a disturbing experience, and you can badly second guess yourself at this point. You might start to create new chapters that don't really fit into your overall scheme, or you might start stuffing material into chapters where it doesn't really belong, just so it doesn't go to waste, or just so you can prove that you really know what you're talking about and haven't left any stone unturned.

What I always do is create a file called Not Sure Where.doc. As before, the purpose is to give yourself flexibility — a provisional organizational structure. You're admitting that you don't know at the moment where this stuff will go, but you're not throwing it away — in fact, you're identifying it as something to be aware of and not forget when the time comes to put the whole thing to bed. And that's just what happens: by the time I've gotten into the writing phase of a book and I'm pretty sure where everything is going, I periodically open up Not Sure Where (which by now may be as much as 50–125 KB in size) to make sure I haven't forgotten anything that should go in with what I'm writing.

The sad fact is that you never use everything you've collected. The Not Sure Where file often has some of the tastiest morsels, but that doesn't mean they have to go in the book, or even that they should go in the book. They were just part of all that you had to know in order to write such a good book. Couldn't have done it without them.

One final piece of good news, though. The great thing about the Web is that you can make good use of your leftovers. I was loosely involved in a BBC television project about the guitar, and when the series finally aired, the producer spent weeks uploading amazing or hilarious clips that never made it into the broadcast series. The web material was, in its fragmented way, just as interesting and a great deal more voluminous than what the TV viewers saw. You can do just the same with some of the stories you've unearthed, but couldn't use in the book. Nothing needs to be wasted.

KEEP A JOURNAL

Let's face it, I'm a guy, and a Brit, and as such I was trained never to talk about feelings — so journaling did not come naturally to me. For half my life, my instinct was to make sure I kept my feelings secret even from myself.

All that changed when I read Virginia Woolf's *A Writer's Diary*. In a sense the book cheats a little, because in editing down his deceased wife's diary by selecting excerpts that referred to her writing life, Leonard Woolf gave it a focus and apparent purpose the writer never intended.

Yet this was a creative act in itself, because Leonard Woolf invented a new (but soon to become quite familiar) genre: what I have my students call a writer's journal. In other words, a papery companion in which the writer notes down his or her thoughts, ideas, questions and feelings about writing, the writing life, or the particular writing project in progress.

Whenever I start working on a book, I start a writer's journal specifically on the subject of that book.

What goes into that journal? Several things.

- Notes from my research
- Interesting conversations I've had on the subject of the book

- Questions that have occurred to me
- Musings as a result of those questions

Here's an example from the time when I was carving the first exhibition of Endangered Alphabets. I hoped to make 10-12 carvings, and I found examples of about eight straight away. Then I began to develop a wish list based on my research on the website Omniglot.com and a variety of other sources. This is a fairly typical example of my journal entries, in that it combines note-taking with question-asking, thinking-out-loud, and task-setting.

Ranjana

Omniglot.com: The Ranjana script is one of the many alphabets derived from the Brahmi script. It developed during the 11th century AD and was used until the mid-20th century in India and Nepal by the Newar people to write the Newar language.

Tibetans use this script, which they call Lantsa, for writing the Sanskrit titles of books which have been translated from Sanskrit to Tibetan, and for decoration in temples and mandalas. Many original Sanskrit manuscripts, written in Lantsa, were preserved in the old monasteries of Tibet but most of these were destroyed following the Chinese take-over.

Questions: Is this the same thing as Newari? Why am I having such difficulty finding someone who knows Ranjana? Is it just because it is rare, or am I asking the wrong questions, or of the wrong people?

By the way: the Chinese burning of Tibetan monasteries is further evidence of the close and powerful connection between a religion and its script. In a sense, though, this evidence goes the other way: it shows that if you can sever the connection between a people and the spiritual script, you may be able to drive a wedge between that people and their religious and cultural identity, which is presumably what the Chinese wanted to do.

If the manuscripts were burned, maybe I can find photographs of the decorations? Of course, I'd have no idea what the script says, so I'd be back where I started.

Maybe Mark Turin knows about this through his research in the Himalayas....

Not all my writer's journal entries are so coherent, of course, and some are much more anxious, pessimistic, angry, or just plain boring. The point is not the content — the point is the process. The writer's journal allows you to chew over what you've been reading and thinking and talking about, and to convert that cud into words. The very act of writing keeps our mental nose sniffing around the subject, trying to make sense of it. It may not look like an organizing principle — after all, many of these entries are fragmentary or even, by the time I come to read them, nonsensical — but in fact the act of writing organizes fleeting and half-glimpsed mental flashes into the relatively stable medium of words, and for that we should be grateful.

The trick is not to be too grateful. By the time I've finished work on a book the writer's journal may be a hundred pages long or more, but in only in the case of *Endangered Alphabets* did I use much of the journal, and then only by coming clean and acknowledging that the whole book was essentially the journal I kept while carving the first Endangered Alphabets exhibition.

No, in most cases I trawl through my writer's journal and barely use any of it — a sentence here, a paragraph there. Fact is, by the time I've got around to the writing stage of the book, the writer's journal has done most of its work already. It has helped me through the not-all-who-wander-are-lost stage, during which my sense of direction was still largely guesswork, and got me to the point where I know roughly what I'm going to write.

THE PLASMA STATE

Here's an interesting question: what is a book before it's written? I ask this because it's really a question about how we think, and more specifically how we think about writing, and most specifically how we thinking about writing a book.

And as a first-time author, the greatest danger you face is your own misunderstandings about writing. We're going to come back to this time and again, like marking crosses on the minefield map.

Whether you've been thinking about your book idea for two months or for thirty years (and two of my most successful books were on subjects I'd been thinking about for thirty years, but the idea of writing about them had somehow never crossed my mind), at this early stage your book is still a loose, wriggling pile of thoughts.

As such, the whole enterprise is very light on its feet. It's like a plasma, a cloud of charged particles. It is subject to certain forces — your own interest, your attention — but is remarkably, almost alarmingly free to move all over the place.

This is why it's much easier to think about writing a novel than to write a novel — because all of those charged particles are free to wander, and everything is light and easy and uncommitted. The hard work hasn't yet really started.

Here's my advice: enjoy this phase. Allow yourself to explore this cloud, this plasma, because at no time will you be as free as you are at the moment. Even if, as I say, you've been thinking about the subject for thirty years, that doesn't mean you've been actively exploring it as a writer, and I can guarantee the ideas you've had are less than ten percent of the ideas you'll have had by the time you've finished writing.

One of the great pleasures of writing is to allow yourself just to sit in the middle of that plasma and look around. If you're writing fiction, for example, one of the great pleasures is to imagine a scene. You know Character A is going to be meeting Character B in a particular place, so you look around, see who else is there. Your imagination (enriched, I hope, by your research) is creating furniture and people, colors and smells, and it's just wonderful. When I'm working on a novel I feel as though I'm in my own favorite company.

Equally, when you're writing nonfiction, there's a slightly different cloud of ideas and possibilities. Here's an example. When I was hitchhiking across America for the second time, a subject I knew I was going to write about, I was in Nebraska on the interstate, in the cab of a truck. I saw a sign pointing toward a low range of hills in the distance on the left, saying "Massacre Canyon." What massacre? I had no idea.

At once that phrase became one of the charged particles in my mind. For the next ten miles, and in a less focused sense for the next month, it kept coming back to me. The massacre could hardly have been the slaughter of a group of Indians by settlers or the army — the word "massacre" implies a transgression and a guilt that would never have occurred to the white victors. Perhaps some whites had been massacred by Indians — but then again, it's unlikely the spot would have been memorialized in a name.

The question darted around my mind, lighting up every time some other tragic aspect of Indian history, all too common in the West, showed up beside the road. In the end, I got back home and looked it up, to find that a group of Pawnee, hunting buffalo, were massacred by a larger force of Sioux. So that explained most of the question of what we memorialize, but there are always more forces at work in the plasma than you might think. The massacre was one factor in the Pawnee's decision to move to a reservation, in Oklahoma; it also reinforced in the collective white consciousness the fact that the Sioux were savage and dangerous. The name, then, became a political weapon, mutely arguing for the continued army presence in the West, and continued military action against the Sioux.

This plasma state, then, is wonderfully creative. And while you're in it, you should make the most of it. Issue yourself a challenge to make sure you make the most of this untethered, exploratory state of mind.

One of the fascinating things about nonfiction is that if you ask good questions and you're diligent about your research and your thinking, and you work on a book for two years, you may be asking questions that nobody else in the history of the world has ever asked.

Likewise, if you throw out the easy conventions of fiction, you may lead yourself to tell a story that has never been told.

That should be your ambition. You might not have answers to all of those questions, but simply to ask them is an exciting thing for you and an exciting thing for the reader. It charges you, it galvanizes you.

This is the force that is going to sustain you as you keep working on this book — and, trust me, if you're going to be working on it for two to five years, it had better sustain you. If you regard yourself as just plodding through a predetermined path, whether it's a plot of a set of questions in nonfiction or a plot you've already mapped out, then you're not charging yourself up. You're not giving yourself the motivation to continue on this long process. You want to always allow yourself the opportunity to be excited about what you're doing.

What makes the difference between great nonfiction and ordinary nonfiction and, I'd argue, the difference between great fiction and ordinary fiction is the breadth of the context. A great book asks huge, often unanswerable questions, but at least you're tackling those big questions. Being in the plasma state is undirected (and can be addictive), but it's also liberating and energizing, both now and for the rest of the project. Make the most of it.

IN THE THICK OF THINGS

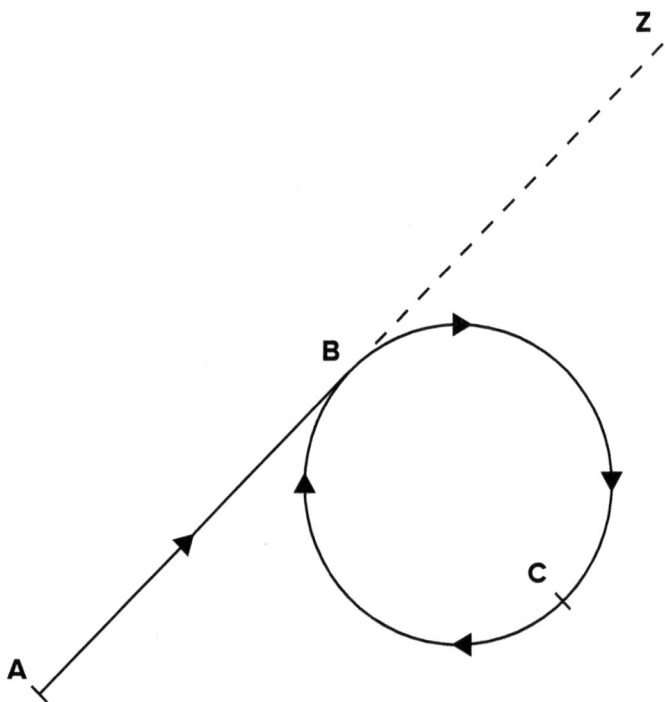

A   You set out, full of high hopes, good
       intentions, and mistaken assumptions

B   The writing starts to take on its own life,
       and a direction, of its own

C   Chaos. Crisis. Catastrophe.

Z   Where you thought you were heading

IN PRAISE OF TANGENTS

1. GEOMETRY WITHOUT TEARS

A lot of writers, especially inexperienced writers, believe or assume that writing is a linear process — that is, it follows a straight line. You start at A and you write on through to Z.

Sooner or later, they have a disturbing experience. They start writing at A, and they're heading along toward Z when at some point (which we're going to call B) they find themselves getting interested in a particular aspect of their subject that catches their attention and their imagination. They write more energetically, more enjoyably, and in fact they're so engrossed in this particular line of thought that they barely notice they're not following their original plan.

After a while they stop and look around, so to speak, and realize to their horror that they're at point C, heading away from Z. If asked to describe what has happened, they say, "I went off on a tangent."

Point C suddenly starts to look as though it stands for Crisis, or even Catastrophe. At this point the inexperienced writer panics and typically does one of three things: (i) abandon the project altogether and try a different topic; (ii) throw away all the writing between

B and C, albeit reluctantly, as when they were writing that stuff it really felt as though they were on a roll; or (iii) find some bizarre and awkward short cut that allows them to jump directly from C to Z. Sure it's lame, and even bad writing, but after all, the goal was to get to Z and, dammit, they're going to get there come hell or high water.

Yet here's the thing: writing is not linear; writing is, in fact, all about being on a roll. Once you find the emotional core of your subject, it catches you in its gravity and you race around it, full of energy, until you exhaust your subject or yourself and collapse like a little dust-devil.

What's more, you may well find you can go back to the first few paragraphs — the line A–B — and just throw them away. They will probably seem much stiffer and more awkward than what followed. Their only purpose, in fact, was to help you discover what you really wanted to write about. Keep the good stuff, the roll.

Now we come to the true genius of this diagram. Remember what our author said: "I'm going off on a tangent"?

But what is a tangent, exactly? It's a straight line that touches a circle at just one point. Look at our diagram. *The true tangent is the line A–Z.*

In other words, if you start out trying to write from beginning to end, you're already heading down the wrong path. Writing is about exploration and discovery. It's about discovering your subject, and discovering yourself.

2. THINGS CHANGE

You've started the project and things are getting going. You've done some research. You may have written bits and pieces of paragraphs, some notes, maybe some of which you're pretty convinced you're going to use. The single most important thing to realize in any creative project, though, is that things change.

By definition, this is a creative project, which means your ideas will evolve as you go, even if you're working on something that's very factual. Any journalist will tell you the story changes as you get more information; your understanding of the situation becomes richer and more complex. That's what makes good writing. Likewise, any good novelist will tell you some of the characters just started growing by themselves, taking over the plot as they grew. In that sense change is the same thing as development. But this is, for most first-time authors, a very scary proposition.

You start out thinking, "There's a lot of work here, but I just have to keep slogging from A–Z and I'm done." As you go from A to B, though, after a while you start to realize you're not actually heading towards Z. You're heading towards B flat minor.

This is no longer a narrow and linear process, which is good, because a narrow and linear book is not an interesting book. But it means that you're probably going to reach a crisis point, maybe even several crisis points, where you go, "Oh my God, am I going off on a tangent? Am I losing track of what I'm doing? Am I taking on a subject that's now too big? Do I have writer's block?"

You do not have writer's block. As we already discovered, writer's block doesn't exist. What is happening is you're simply asking yourself the wrong questions.

Let's look at some specific examples of how this may show up in your consciousness. I'll give you a good example. In 2002 I was sent by *National Geographic* to India to write about the monsoon for a story on weather forecasting. I went to India because I had read, and was under the impression, that the monsoon forecast is the greatest act of weather forecasting in the world. In a light monsoon, there is widespread drought, hundreds of thousands of people and cattle die of starvation and heat; it's a disaster. But if it's a heavy monsoon, people drown, there are all kinds of mudslides and disease epidemics, and hundreds of thousands of cattle drown. I had always wanted to go to India, and this was my way of persuading an editor to send me and pay for me to go there.

When I got there, what I discovered was that nobody in India pays the slightest attention to the weather forecast, first of all because it comes from the government, so straightaway they don't trust it, and secondly, their attitude is "There isn't really much we can do. We cannot stop it raining."

Meanwhile, it turned out that methods that the India Meteorological Department were using to predict the monsoon were deeply flawed and produced results that were actually not particularly accurate. So suddenly, what had been a simple task — go to India, watch the monsoon come ashore and then interview a couple of meteorologists — was much more complicated. In fact I went through some considerable panic, because in addition to the story getting more complicated, I also got banned from every single meteorological department in the country because they were under the mistaken impression that I was making a film.

But what I discovered was in many respects much more interesting than the original story, and in fact it became the book *Thirty Percent Chance of Enlightenment.* After interviewing ordinary people all across southern India, it struck me that I had stumbled on a much broader and deeper question, which was how a society copes with philosophical uncertainty.

If the massive, dramatic uncertainty of monsoon season hangs over you every year, what do you do about it? By banking on chaos, so to speak, the Indians have developed some remarkably sane attitudes toward weather. I interviewed one man whose mother had a mattress and a canoe in her attic. If the rain covered the lower floor of her house, she went up and slept on the mattress. If it rose to the attic, she launched the canoe through the window and paddled away.

It's almost a metaphor for writing: the trick is to expect change, and be ready for it.

Easier said than done, of course. In my own case, I took a lot of good notes, and waited until I could figure out what the new story was about. It took months. You probably have to allow yourself that time. If you don't, you're going to rush to the conclusion that the book isn't working, that you don't know how to push on to Z, and you'll end up staring at the keyboard thinking you have the dreaded writer's block.

Imagine that the work you're doing on your book is an apprenticeship. You're learning about your subject, but you're also learning how to write about your subject, whether you're a fiction writer or a nonfiction writer.

The single biggest mistake that you, dear reader, can make is to assume that this whole process you're about to undertake is easy and you should be able knock it off without too much trouble — because then, when you do run into trouble, you're going to think that there's something profoundly wrong.

What you have to assume is that you're learning something large and complex and demanding; *you're capable of doing it but you're not capable of doing it right away.* Give yourself time to figure all this stuff out. If you don't give yourself that time, you will kill yourself. Things will change. The subject will change. All of this is absolutely business as usual.

GLOWING FRAGMENTS

If you follow the process I've suggested, there is no "starting to write" point, like the writer in the movie with the blank sheet in the typewriter — and consequently, there's no "starting to write" stress.

If you move through the research-and-accumulation phase (actually, the term "hunter-gatherer" works pretty well) I recommend, before you know it you have already accumulated a fair number of choice words, phrases, sentences, even paragraphs. This is what we in the trade call writing.

I take that back. That was a bad sentence — not only because it was a cheap laugh, but because in the trade there is very real debate about what constitutes writing, and how to go about starting it.

One point of view is championed by the well-known author Anne Lamott, whose *Bird By Bird* has become pretty much a standard work on the writing process. I have a great deal of respect for her and her writing, but in one important respect she and I differ completely. She advocates writing what she calls "a shitty first draft" — in other words, no matter how much you dislike what you're writing, you plough through, finish that draft, and then go back and write successively better second, third, fourth, and eighty-eighth drafts.

The shitty-first-draft approach, as she says, helps get around a problem faced by many first time authors: perfectionism. Worry each sentence to death and you'll never finish your book.

On the other hand, painfully writing page after page of shitty prose can also worry you to death. It turns writing into drudgery, and saddles you with two downstream problems. One: All the time you're writing that first draft you have to maintain the belief that you can improve it. Two: You are then faced with the problem of making bad writing better, which is by no means as straightforward as it might sound. I have what I think is a better method.

I call it Glowing Fragments.

In fact, you may have been practicing it already. A glowing fragment is any word or sequence of words that you have coined or copied (from your research, for quotation) because it says exactly what you want it to say. It is the opposite of a shitty first draft: it is a tiny piece of a draft that is anything but shitty. You like it, you are proud of it, it reinforces your sense that you're a writer, and it gets a very, very small but probably important part of the job done.

What a glowing fragment doesn't have that a shitty first draft does have is structure. You don't yet know where it's going to go, or what will go before and after it. And that can get disconcerting if you let it.

On the other hand, all that shitty first draft does have to offer is structure, and that structure may be deceiving. If you write something dull or clumsy on the assumption that at least you have created a backbone for your book, you may discover that if you stick to that structure, you can't write the less-shitty drafts you were hoping for.

My advice, then, is to write what you can write well, what you enjoy writing — even if what you write is only a paragraph, or even a sentence. Dull writing begets dull writing, but exciting writing begets exciting writing: when you come back and read that paragraph, it may well strike sparks in your imagination. The fragments grow and merge. In my experience, at least, the problem of having to fit them all together is easier than you expect, and easier than trying to turn shit into gold.

And as you make the transition into the writing phase (which is a much gentler way of looking at it than "When you start writing..."), you can practice very much the same technique. If you know what comes next, write what comes next. If not, write what most interests you, what most taps on your shoulder and tells you to write it. Every time I write a book, I usually work on at least half-a-dozen chapters at more or less the same time — a section here, a paragraph there. (This book is no exception.) If I write what I'm interested in at that moment, then the writing itself is interesting.

Fiction may need to be somewhat more sequential than non-fiction, but even in fiction you can jog ahead to a setting you know you're going to use, even if you haven't figured out exactly what action is going to take place, and have a good time describing the surroundings, the smells, the colors. The jump ahead gives you, literally, a change of scenery.

What's more, Anne Lamott herself quotes the novelist E.L. Doctorow as saying, "Writing a novel is like driving a car at night. You can see only as far as your headlights, but you can make the whole trip that way." In other words, take it easy on yourself. Look ahead, write a little, pull over for coffee. Write those glowing fragments.

This method also takes into account what might be called the mental physiology of writing. Nobody can write forever — in fact, not many people can write more than a few pages at a time. The mental effort is exhausting. And if you've told yourself you have to keep on plugging away at that chapter until it's done, sooner or later you're going to find yourself both out of ideas and exhausted, yet believing you have to keep going. That's a terrible and dangerous combination.

If, on the other hand, you're allowing yourself to create glowing fragments, you write in manageable chunks. The reason why the farming landscape of New England looks like a patchwork is that, traditionally, each field was the size a man could plough in a day. At the end of the day, then, just as the man was getting exhausted, there was a stopping point and a sense of achievement. Personally, my writing limit is somewhere between 45 minutes and an hour, and I've adopted the habit of not even trying to tackle an acreage of text that will take longer than that. Write the fragment that is glowing in your mind, stop, make a cup of tea, throw the laundry into the dryer.

Right now, at this early stage, it doesn't matter that you can't see exactly where it's all going. Just enjoy the journey. No book was written in a day. Settle in. Get comfortable. Allow your best self to come to the table, or the desk, and see what your best self has to say.

MODUS OPERANDI

If you're like almost every first-time author, by the time you're well into your project you'll discover that your working method — your *modus operandi*, or, as they say in the cop-and-serial-killer shows, your M.O. — will have changed.

The project will be taking more time than you thought. It will involve more money that you thought, because you're having to make phone calls, buy documents, travel to places to find stuff out. Certain things that you thought would be really easy are going to be harder than you expected. Some things you thought were going to be hard might actually turn out to be pretty easy. But in a broader sense, how the book fits in with your life as a whole may well have changed.

If, for example, you have a very supportive partner, and that person understands that you write best from midnight until 3 a.m., that's wonderful and I congratulate you on your good fortune. But after you've been working on this book project for, say, six to nine months, your partner may have had a change of mind, and is now throwing dark looks in your direction and muttering what sound suspiciously like curses.

So it's probably time to metaphorically put the pen down

and step back and ask yourself those really good writer-process questions. Under what circumstances do I do my best writing? How much time should I really be spending on this project each week? Do I need to revise my deadlines?

And those questions may involve really significant changes elsewhere in your life, such as talking to your partner and saying, "Look, I'm trying to get this done but there's just too much noise around the house, too many distractions. I think I need to spend a week on my own just working on this."

On the other hand, for some people retreating to write in solitude may be the very worst thing. For some writers, when they're on their own, and there's nothing else to do but write, they feel as if they're under terrible pressure to produce, and being alone makes that worse. You've got to ask yourself what's best for you.

For me, I love writing in cafes and in airports. So if I needed to put in a bunch of work and somebody suggested I spend three weeks in a cabin in the woods, I would go completely crazy.

In every sense, you've got to be comfortable. You can't be working under adverse physical circumstances where the light is bad and the surface is isn't even, because you're going to lose concentration, develop a stiff neck. You've got to ask yourself, where is my good working surface?

For myself, the answer is *anywhere but on a plane*. I can't tell you how many stiff necks, sore backs, and sets of tired shoulders I've developed as a result of cramming a laptop under my chin, flinching every time the person in the seat ahead slams backwards into my screen.

It has also taken me a ridiculously long time — decades, in fact — to notice that, as a tall guy, I lean forward when I write on anything but a deliberately elevated surface, and once again the stiff neck, the tired shoulders.

If I have one more piece of advice, it is never try to write in the office. And by "the office" I mean anywhere where people may have access to you (by phone, by email, in person) and may legitimately demand your attention at a moment's notice. About fifteen years ago I went through a period when I didn't have a decent working space at home, and I was also teaching a fair amount at the university, so I tried to work at my office desk. It was like being pecked to death by sparrows. If I got fifteen minutes' writing done at a stretch I was lucky, and as a result I bitterly resented the intrusion. I love teaching, and my students, but writing is like dreaming: you just don't want to be jarred into a more mundane state of focus.

So much for places to write, or rather not to write. What about times?

Everyone's biorhythms vary, but we may all have one thing in common: the altered state of consciousness in the middle of the night. That strange loss of imaginative inhibition often leads to a wonderful, even bizarre intermingling between conscious idea and dream, and we are furnished, willy-nilly, with all kinds of images and associations to add to what we're writing. I've often deliberately made use of this unpredictable but amazing source by putting a blank book or pad of paper next to me so I could scribble down words and phrases in the middle of the night — without turning on the light and ruining the midnight moment of inspiration. Experience as a film reviewer in a dark movie theater had taught me, by the way, that one scribbled line obliterates another beneath it with remarkable effectiveness, so I wrote with so much space between one line and the next that I captured as few as half a dozen lines per page.

In the end, we writers have to face a dilemma. We want to preserve everything we write, ideally in digital form, because we can then edit it, cut it and paste it, and generally act as though our slightest verbal effusion is priceless. I'm as guilty of this as anyone. And that tells us we should write on a computer. In fact, it implies we should write at any available opportunity, which in turn implies we should write on a laptop. In fact, just to prove how susceptible I am to this belief, even after all my books, *even after everything I've just written*, I am in fact writing this on a laptop, on a plane.

Shoot me now.

Yet I can't deny that my best writing is done longhand, on a nice thick legal pad or even in a nice thick lined hardback journal. Something about the luxurious feeling of the good paper, or the slower and more organic act of writing by hand — my entire relationship with my creative mind changes. I think more slowly, more expansively, more like a poet.

What prevents me from writing like this all the time (rather than when I'm traveling, especially as a travel writer)? Simply the fact that I'll have to type it all into my computer when I'm done. Yet even this is no excuse, because experience teaches any writer that his or her writing improves with, and in fact needs, repeated scrutiny: the more times our writing passes under our eyes, the better. The process of typing up our handwritten draft is a valuable editing stage — yet all of us, myself included, look for ways to avoid it.

BACK UP. BACK UP. BACK UP.

The third most important thing you can do as a writer working on a book-length project is to back up your work. The second most important thing is to back up your work, and the most important thing to do, of course, is to back up your work.

When I'm creating new text, I save after every paragraph. I do not rely on Autosave. I also don't rely on my own computer, so I'll save to Dropbox, and if you don't know Dropbox, look it up. I will often email myself what I've just done so it's saved on a server rather than on the computer.

When the first-year students come in and say, "Oh, my computer crashed and I've lost everything that I've done," I say, "Good. That's terrible right now, but that's the only thing that is going to prevent something much worse happening later."

I've had a computer crash through no fault of my own and I lost the first four chapters of book. I also know a Pulitzer-finalist poet who was invited by a publisher to produce his life's best work for a Collected Poems and as he was editing it, he suffered a crash and lost months and months of work.

Frankly, when that happens, it's your fault. It's within your power to back that stuff up, and you need to take that seriously. You can back up to an external hard drive, back up to another server, just keep on backing up. The more you write, the more you need to back up, because the more there is to lose.

Having said that, if you do lose everything, one of the extremely painful but very educational experiences that comes with this is that if you have to rewrite something from memory, no matter how much you hate doing it, that revision will be better than the original.

As you sit down, cursing, to the task of reconstructing everything you have lost, you only remember the most interesting and important stuff. You want to get this excruciatingly tedious process over with as soon as possible, so you're also editing down to what really matters.

No matter how much you may have come up with all kinds of pretty little phrases here and there, what you really want is the important stuff. If you had a really, really good 300 page book and you edited it down to 250 pages, that would be a better book. Sorry.

So it's not the worst thing in the world to lose some text. It hurts like hell, and you really don't want to do it. But you've just got to sit down and redo it as soon as possible. Obviously you allow yourself to swear and curse and kick things first. That goes without saying. But then when you rewrite that missing text, it will be better.

TRANSMUTATION

Transmutation is a term from alchemy. It is used to describe what happens when a substance undergoes a radical change from one state to another.

Your material, right now, is undergoing a transmutation. When you started, there wasn't a book at all, of course: there was a flickering mental activity potentially connected in intangible ways with all kinds of information both deep inside yourself and out in the world, much of it not yet encountered or considered.

Since then, you've started gathering more ideas and converting them into words, and those words are now on paper, or in your computer, or perhaps on a whiteboard. Some are individual facts, numbers, phrases, tiny fragments that have occurred to you, or you've found in other sources. Maybe you have them filed neatly in various folders, maybe they're scribbled on sticky notes that you have stuck up all over the place.

It's possible some of this stuff has been transmuted into more complex clusters of words. If individual words are simple, single-celled organisms, the kinds that inhabited the early days of life on the Earth, you may also have gathered or created more sentient life forms. Perhaps you've found an entire paragraph someone wrote and you've said *This is gold dust. I'm going to quote this entire paragraph.* Perhaps you've spontaneously written a paragraph in your journal that now, looking over these emerging organisms, you really like. If you're writing a screenplay or a novel, you may have written some dialogue.

Here's my warning, and my advice. The only danger facing you is *your own misguided sense of how writing happens.*

If you're dismayed that these pieces aren't all sequential, or aren't all coming together, you may think that a real writer would be moving steadily through chapters one, two, three, and wouldn't be surrounded by all this mess, and if you start thinking like that you may question your abilities as a writer, and give up. That would be a terrible mistake, and a tragedy because it could have been averted.

This gradual assembling of what may look like hopeless disconnected odds and ends — *this is exactly how good writing evolves.* This is how the mind works, especially if it's working on a complex subject. And most books, simply because of their length and the reader's needs, tackle complex subjects. You have to allow your writing to work the way your mind works, not the way a computer works, or a train. It's your mind that will make sense of this whole thing, not your writing. Your writing will only ever be as coherent and as interesting as your thinking.

As a first-time author, you may not be used to thinking of the raw materials of writing. You may be used to thinking of writing as something that's done or not done. Say, for example, you've been writing short stories or magazine articles, stuff that comes to you fairly easily. You have an idea for a story, you pound it out and it's done. It's maybe 1,500 words, or 3,000 words. You have a pretty good idea even before you start writing how it'll all fit together; you come up with a good idea for a lead or opening, you maybe change your mind a couple of times about the ending; you're done.

You can't go about writing a book that way, and you can't go about assuming that book writers write that way, so if you can't write your book that way, you're not a book writer. As I said, your main danger is your own misguided sense of how writing, especially long-form writing, happens.

The fact is that a long-form text such as a book is made up of lots of small pieces. You absolutely have to understand that. What you're writing is not a book. What you're doing is writing pieces that will become a book.

That process has already started. Look at all those notes and jottings. You are writing. You are writing a book.

To be sure, it can be a little disconcerting because at the moment there's no way of knowing for sure how much you've actually "written." People are going to say to you, "You're writing a book? How's it coming along?" You can't possibly say, "Oh, I've written 36.8 percent of it." Even if the book came out to exactly 100,000 words, and you've actually written 36,800 words so far, you're going to revise it, you're going to mess it around, you're going to rethink at least 5,000 of those 36,800 words. Still, there is always strong temptation to think in those terms: How am I doing? How far have I gone? As if writing were like the fundraiser for the new church steeple, with the big white board outside the church with the thermometer painted on it, the red line going up from one dollar level to the next.

You cannot think in those terms. You have to respect what you've achieved. You've got a glowing, radioactive stockpile of raw material. You're in the transmutation process already. You're putting words into larger groups of words, and you want to start being aware of where they're going to go in their larger structure. Increasingly, you're going to think of yourself in terms of creating text — sentences, paragraphs, sections, eventually even chapters. Sometimes you'll have to leave gaps to be filled later; sometimes you'll have to create transitions (which need to be very, very clear and explicit, for you're taking your readers from one idea to something different along a path they've never trodden); sometimes the sections will miraculously lead from one smoothly into another.

You're in the process of converting something as formless and shapeless as a plasma of ideas into something that is as stable as a clear, organized structure of words. You are assembling the book.

SECRECY OR FEEDBACK?

I have no idea whether you're the kind of writer who works alone, or whether you've been sending every sentence out to everyone you know or pasting chunks on Facebook, or more likely somewhere in between. Whatever the situation, let's think about the pros and cons of feedback.

Some writers swear by the belief, attributed to Hemingway but probably much more ancient, that if you tell anyone what you're writing, your desire to write it will leak out of you like air out of a balloon.

Others subscribe to the starving-writer-in-the-garret belief that a real artist/writer/musician is the only person capable of judging his or her art, and anyone else's opinion is only going to drag the art toward the mainstream, the mundane, the worthless.

Everyone is different, of course, but I can tell you, I've tried writing many different ways, and I subscribe to Keats' observation, "How a solitary life engenders pride and egotism!" It also engenders loneliness, self-doubt, frustration, and desperate experimentation. It sucks.

But really, we're looking at this question the wrong way. Like most black-and-white questions, it sets up a false dichotomy. Let me explain.

One of the differences between an experienced writer and inexperienced writer (and this has very little to do with whether you're published or not) is that the experienced writer, like an experienced musician, has developed a sense of what seems to work.

Let's take an analogy from the world of music. When you're starting out as, say, a lead guitarist, you may have some chords and some licks, but what you haven't really learned is *what is going to get people to stand up and cheer.* So you're constantly in danger of second-guessing yourself.

You may have mastered some really tasty rockabilly licks, but you decide to play them through eight different pedals so the result is just too distorted for people to dance to. So you go off and practice on your own until your fingertips are spade-shaped and your skin has taken on this Gollum-like pastiness. After six months you can play these unbelievable solos that go on for 45 minutes, but people just get up and walk out. So you storm off the stage calling the audience philistines who don't appreciate great music. (For those of you who don't know much about guitar, believe me, this happens.)

The problem is neither with your playing nor with your audience. In a sense, the problem is that there is no bridge between the two parties involved. It's that you haven't yet learned, by long and often painful experience, what you've got that people want.

As a writer, especially an inexperienced writer, you don't yet have that assurance that comes with experience, and consequently your principal danger is that you will be afraid that *people won't be interested in what you're writing.* This fear leads to all kinds of unfortunate and unhelpful tactics.

Tactic One: you dash through your material, fiction or non-fiction, as quickly as possible so as not to bore your reader. This leads to two problems, one at each end. Your reader gets a hasty, superficial text that has no twists and turns, no richness of detail. And you, the writer, don't get to enjoy the process of exploring your material and your ideas. Your main emotion is dread.

Tactic Two: you keep apologizing for yourself, explaining and justifying your work, until the reader just wants you to shut up.

Tactic Three: you slice off whole sections of yourself, believing that the reader is a kind of Joe Friday on *Dragnet*, and wants just the facts, or just the story. You may have all kinds of richness of experience you manage to overlook completely.

In my own case I wrote almost an entire novel without any humor at all — despite the fact that humor makes up about 35 percent of my psyche — because I was convinced that great fiction had to be serious, and the reader wouldn't want my humor. Seven years later I was hired by National Public Radio as, essentially, a humorist. Twelve years later I started work on a new novel, about 35 percent of which is intended to be funny.

The only way to develop the confidence that you know how to write, and that people like your writing, is *to give people a chance to like what you write.*

Experienced writers have spent some considerable time getting feedback, and weighing that feedback. They've learned that at least 10 percent of the population is going to hate anything that they write. At least another 10 percent is going to have no interest in anything that they write. (And when I say 10 percent, it may be as high as 70 percent.) But you're not writing for 100 percent of the population. You're writing for the readers who potentially like what you write.

To a first-time author this feels horribly risky, of course. But if you don't take those risks, and especially if you buy into that old myth about a real writer being someone who is so committed to his work that he shuts himself in a leaky attic and engages in his art for, oh, a decade — well, then, things can go horribly wrong.

I had a writing student a few years ago who was a committed fantasy novelist. He worked on his fiction for years and years, from high school until he was senior in college, at which point he finally showed it to one of my colleagues and me. It was 600 pages long. It was the labor of a young lifetime.

My colleague and I read it, and our hearts sank. The first 200 pages were all exposition. Eventually we recommended he throw out the first 200 pages, then cut about 50 percent of the text between pages 200 and 400 as he was still just finding his stride, and then the last 200 pages were actually pretty good. If he had brought reliable, interested, knowledgeable people in earlier, he would have saved himself an awful lot of grief.

Having said that, one of the pleasures of writing is seeing or hearing about your reader's first spontaneous response, when they've read a chapter or the whole book and they go, wow! Consequently, if you are talking in public about every single thing you write, you are indeed in danger of letting the air out of the balloon. The novelty and the exploration, the fun of it — those are some of the things that make us want to write. If you use up that novelty by telling everybody about your book-in-progress, then when it comes time to sit down and write, it's just not as interesting or as exciting to you. You need to strike a balance.

In my case, I very rarely tell people what I'm going to write, except in the broadest sense: I'm going to do a book on so and so. Sometimes I'll say, "I've got to tell you this one amazing little detail," but even so I'll probably only do that maybe once. I want that story to be fresh when I'm writing it.

On the other hand, I think you've got to let others in on what you're writing. You're still an inexperienced writer. This is still your apprenticeship. You're learning on the job, and what you're learning is something huge and complicated. You need as much help as you can get, and as much well-founded confidence as you can develop over time.

TWO HEADS ARE BETTER THAN ONE (SOMETIMES)

At least half of the projects that pass through our hands at the Champlain College Publishing Initiative start out or end up as some kind of collaboration. In some cases a writer is working with an illustrator, especially in the field of children's books or graphic novels. In others, two writers are working together to bring different skills or areas of knowledge together. As we move farther into the digital publishing age, we're seeing writers working with programmers and designers on apps or web-based projects.

The digital age has, in fact, made possible an almost infinite form of collaboration: crowdsourcing. Here's an example. We asked Alisha Durgin, a sophomore in our Public Relations program, to write a *Short, Sweet Guide to Press Releases*. She had never written a book before; in fact, she'd never written a press release before she started as out publicist for the publishing initiative.

On the one hand, this made her the perfect candidate to learn by doing, and write about the act of discovery as it was taking place. On the other hand, she had no stockpile of press releases to draw on, and no depth or breadth of experience that would help her map out the most important issues to address.

So she called in collaborators. She joined LinkedIn, signed

up with a number of groups of publicity/marketing/writing professionals, and posted a request: If you had to give one piece of advice to someone just learning to write press releases, what would it be?

The professionals on LinkedIn responded at once, almost swamping her with advice, stories, painful lessons, links to various resources and examples of press releases that illustrated valuable points. Within a week she had been joined, briefly, by 50 collaborators, and in return for their help she promised to credit them in the book and include links to their websites.

For a lot of first-time authors, though, the whole concept of writing a book is so personal an act of self-expression that any form of collaboration poses difficult issues. Who is really in charge? Who has creative control? What if I don't like my collaborator's work?

Even to think in these terms can set up a dangerous dynamic: without realizing it, you assume that your collaborator is working for you, or doing your bidding, or working on your schedule. That kind of thinking is almost certain to lead to misunderstandings, and to the whole being less than the sum of the parts.

Sure, an experienced professional is used to working on someone else's project with a clear set of instructions and a deadline — but if you're a first-time author, your collaborator is more likely to be someone almost as new to this kind of work as yourself, and (more importantly) someone who is getting involved for the creative adventure rather than the hard cash. If you treat that person as your unpaid employee, at the very least they're not going to give themselves over to the full range of their creative and imaginative abilities. At worst, they're going to feel steadily more resentful and distanced from you and your book.

The crucial first step, then, is to talk to each other as equals. To do a lot of talking, in fact. To allow your own vision of the project to be a little elastic, a little open to the creative ideas your collaborator may bring along.

This is likely to make you feel more than somewhat apprehensive, but the truth is, if your potential collaborator suggests all kinds of wild-eyed possibilities, this may be a very useful early sign that the two of you are better off not working together. What's more, this discussion may help that person get a better idea of your own vision, intentions, and aesthetics.

The other discussion to have, as soon as possible, concerns not the what so much as the how and the when.

The single most important question, or at least the most important question you may not think of addressing at this stage, is: how do we work together? No two pairs of collaborators are ever going to work together in exactly the same way, and no pair of collaborators is always going to agree about what to create or even how to go about creating.

Should you each go away and work on some aspect of the project and then send each other the results for comment? Should you try to meet face to face on a regular basis? Should you set up a timeline and a to-do list for each of you? Should you have interim deadlines?

Should you restrict your feedback to only the positives? Should you give feedback in writing, or conversationally? Are you even entitled to comment on the work of someone whose field is different to yours, and who is more experienced in that field than you are?

At this stage, the most important thing to do is keep the lines of communication open. Remember, though, that email or text communication is emotionally opaque: it's very, very easy to give the wrong impression. If you can meet in person, so much the better. If not, then use a video call service like Skype, so at least you can see and hear each other's expressions. If you're not sure what feedback or discussion your collaborator will find permissible or likely to be helpful, talk about that.

Bear in mind that your project has a particular audience or readership, and they may have exactly the same unskilled reactions that you do, so the fact that you're not an expert doesn't invalidate your reactions. It just means you may be less skilled at working on the situation to improve those reactions.

In general, then, collaboration is literally a work in progress. Try one method for a couple of weeks, and see how it goes, then talk about it. Above all, remember that a feeling of frustration or friction is simply a sign that some aspect of your method isn't working quite right at that particular moment. It doesn't mean you can't work together, or that the book can't be written.

One other important thing. I'm going to suggest you write out, together, a letter of understanding about who does what by when, who owns what — all those contractual details. Don't say, "Oh, we're friends. We don't need a contract." Don't say, "Oh a contract is going to make everything heavy and legalistic between us." Even if you never actually sign the letter, it will force you to discuss things that need to be agreed upon.

Don't forget that time and money are important elements, and highly combustible. Make sure you explicitly work out a timeline that works for both of you. You can always modify it later, but it's dangerous to have unspoken assumptions.

I'm actually collaborating, right now, on a project with someone who is a wonderfully skilled individual but a terrible communicator, and as a result I never know whether his part of the work is going as planned — so I wrote out a three-point agreement that says that he will communicate with me at least once a week, that if any of our planned meetings needs to be changed he will notify me, and that if I contact him he will respond within 24 hours. Agreements like that may seem a little cold or harsh, but they may also save your sanity and your project.

Ditto money: have you discussed intellectual property, rights, royalties, and so on? Believe me, it is far easier to agree on a collaboration when there is no money at stake than when there is. The closer you get to success — which is presumably what you want — the greater the likelihood of disagreement, tension, even litigation. And then, as they say, the only winners are the lawyers. Even lawyers say that. Discuss the details at the start and you'll avoid problems later.

And here's an example of "problems later." I worked for nine months on a book project in which a writer, who was in the middle of some fascinating and dramatic events, wrote regular email bulletins that I edited and amplified. When we started out, we were both very enthusiastic about the project, as was my agent.

By the time the manuscript was complete, my collaborator was beginning to question some of the fundamentals, and a rift was beginning to open between us — a rift that was made only wider by the responses of the New York editors who saw the book proposal. They were mixed or lukewarm, and explicitly said they liked the (relatively short) sections I'd written, but were much less keen on hers.

The whole thing blew up, and she accused me of sabotaging the project. At that point, even though I had put a lot of work into the book, I knew it would be best to cut my losses, hand everything over to her to do with as she wished, and walk away.

Pretty much my only real piece of advice to you both is to remember that, as it's an adventure rather than a predictable and familiar commute, collaboration is bound to include all kinds of new and unexpected landscapes. It's pretty much guaranteed you'll get lost every so often! The trick is not to be daunted when the map turns out to have been eaten by termites.

LIFE GETS IN THE WAY

It's always sad to see writers engaged in a perfectly feasible project who've made it unfeasible by saying that unless they've finished by a particular date, they've failed. Or, just as sad, to see writers feeling more and more pressured — to the point of grinding to a halt — because they've set themselves unrealistic timelines.

Back in the very beginning of this book, I recommended you set yourself a schedule or timeline, one that operates both on the macro scale of the project as a whole and on the micro scale of a daily or weekly schedule of writing. By now I'd be very surprised if you don't find yourself needing to revise that schedule, those expectations.

Which is not to say you can't write, or you're managing your time badly. Again, it has to do with the nature of a large project full of new demands and uncertainty. When I was writing *Signs of Life*, the book about hospice, and I, like the rest of my family, was navigating the unfamiliar and disturbing territory of dealing with someone in the process of dying, I wrote, "The novelty alone can kill you." As a first time author, the novelty alone can cause enough confusion and self-doubt to make you stop dead.

Right now you may need to make one or more of several kinds of adjustment. You may need to adjust your working methods; you may need to adjust your timeline; you may need to adjust your content.

Let's take the last first, as it's the easiest to understand. One of my students, after graduation, was hired to help an author writing a major non-fiction book. Her job was to do research, and to organize the research materials the author had already gathered. Almost at once it became clear that the job was impossible. The writer was not only hopelessly disorganized — she could have done something about that — but was so overcommitted to the research phase that she was compulsively gathering more and more material and getting farther and farther away from actually writing anything. In the end, the book missed multiple deadlines and then collapsed. It became not a book but a (messy) archive.

Your schedule can prevent that. Like a change in the weather, it can help signal a change in the seasons of your book. Time to start moving from the research phase into the organizing-and-writing phase. Time to finish up this draft and stand back to look at the work as a whole. It's what gives your publisher-self a voice, gentle but clear. Let's move on, now.

On the other hand, it's possible you may need to adjust your schedule. Life may have gotten in the way to a degree you could not have predicted. A friend of mine, working on a very manageable book and very much on schedule, had to cope with the illness and death of his wife. Under those circumstances you can't and arguably shouldn't be writing. Something more important is happening — and even if you have a few minutes' respite, your mind is elsewhere, and the words won't come.

So, adjust your schedule. Give yourself breathing space. Recognize that writing is going to demand your presence, your mind working at its best. When will that best be available to you again? Reset your deadline. If you're working with a traditional publisher, the editor will understand (up to a point, at least). Everyone knows that life involves more than just writing.

Let me tell you a teaching tactic I use to try to show my students the survival tactics of the freelance writer. Most of them are really good students, bright and committed, but they still have the working habits of students. If an assignment is due on, say, Friday morning, they'll assume that they'll dig into it on Thursday, and if it takes all night, they'll pull an all-nighter.

The problem with this approach, for a writer, is that you can't tell whether all night will be enough. Your material may simply not be available or malleable enough to get beaten into shape in four or eight hours. So one day I stop class and tell them, "As a writer, you need to get used to thinking of time as being infinitely valuable. That means you need to think in smaller and smaller units of time, and you need to make good use of even the smallest amount of time available to you. So we're going to stop class for the next 15 minutes, and I want you to spend those 15 minutes doing something of value to your current writing project. Doesn't matter what it is. What matters is that you shift mental gears quickly and focus quickly on the task at hand. Go."

If your book is at all behind schedule, you may need to rethink how, when and where you write. You may need to slice your time more thinly. You may get to that author-state in which you inhabit the book and the book inhabits you, and the laundry simply gets done less often.

Hey, there's no getting around it: a book is a major commitment. And because writing, like any art, is unpredictable in both good and bad ways, your task won't fit comfortably into little boxes on your wall calendar. Just to give you an up-to-the-moment illustration: I'm typing this with the laptop resting on a half-finished carving of Mongolian calligraphy, part of my Endangered Alphabets work. We write when we can. We just have to make sure we can.

All this writing work you've taken on, then, may well change not just your work habits but your life. You may have to become that magnificent, annoying, self-involved, brilliant, off-the-beaten-path creature: a writer.

A STRUCTURE EMERGES
FROM THE SWAMP

As your understanding of your subject changes, then your initial sense of the structure needs to change, and if you're a fiction writer, your initial sense of the plot needs to change.

This is why I've been suggesting a *provisional* sense of structure. If you start out by making an outline or a table of contents, that may be a good idea, but largely because it gets you to think about what you want to explore. Now we're in the middle of things, you've been doing some exploring, and you're getting a better sense of what's out there. You are probably going to discover there are other things you need to explore as well that don't fit into your initial outline. And that's the way things go. That's "business as usual."

Equally, you may discover that some of the things that you thought were important are either unavailable or not particularly important compared to certain other things, or you're just not interested in them any more. At this point, you have to bear in mind: What am I trying to achieve? Your goal is not to try to follow your original outline. Your goal is to write the book — which may be a different kind of book than you originally thought. That's fine.

It's always a mistake to have too rigid a concept of structure when you start out. But on the other hand, by the time you've finished

writing the damn thing, it's got to have some kind of structure —
so when does this organizing process happen?

The answer is not that you say, "On April 7, I'm going to figure
out what the structure of this book is." However, now you're in the
middle phase, you want to ask yourself, "What are the major pieces
of this book?"

When I say "major pieces," I'm deliberately not using the terms
"chapters" or "sections." Let me explain. When I was writing the
book on the SARS pandemic, it was clear after about three or
four weeks' research that a certain number of countries, perhaps
a dozen, had had very dramatic and significant brush with SARS:
multiple deaths, huge upheavals in civic society, schools closed, new
hospitals built in rapid time, massive efforts at tracing the various
people who had been infected, or had come in contact with those
who were infected.

Other countries, meanwhile, had suffered less devastation, but
had nevertheless been clearly affected by SARS in significant and
often interesting ways, especially as different countries had adopted
different strategies to try to contain the spread of the virus.

From early on, then, I began thinking I'd have a chapter on
each of the countries that had a major incident, and then perhaps
a wrap-up chapter that acted as a kind of summation of what had
taken place elsewhere. That still didn't answer the question of how
these chapters might be ordered.

A book needs to feel clear and coherent, but it also needs to feel
as though it adds up to something worthwhile. This need is most
obvious in fiction, where we want a novel to grow in intensity and
tension and significance to a climax, and then a resolution. But
a non-fiction book (unless it is simply an assemblage of valuable
information such as a dictionary) benefits from a similar sense of
progress through the chapters, and satisfaction at the end.

With the SARS book, it made sense to give each major country
a chapter, as each suffered differently and tackled the crisis
differently, but a chapter-by-chapter, country-by-country summary

is all outline and no drive. Where's the momentum? Where's the sense of destination?

So I decided to resort to the simplest, oldest structure of all, one that we all used in our elementary school writing (and then had beaten out of us in high school where we were told to organize by topics): I told a story. I used a chronological structure.

A chronological structure is hard to beat. Not only does it make instinctive sense, and is easy to follow (this happened, then this happened) but it respects the fact that actions have consequences (this happened, therefore this happened). And as with a novel, it's not just that events take place; it's that *our understanding grows with each event that takes place.*

At the start of the SARS pandemic, everything was very simple, and dramatic in a very straightforward way: people started dying, and nobody knew why. Three months into the outbreak an incredibly complex mass of information had developed (How does the disease travel? How does it infect people, and how rapidly? Is it a virus, or some other disease organism? Do standard antivirals work against it? How can you quarantine an entire population? Do thermal scanners help identify people with symptoms? Does it help to close schools? And so on, and so on), and an equally complex series of decisions were being made and strategies were being tried. This complexity grew as the outbreak grew.

It makes sense, then, to follow the human story, and to have the reader learn as the world learned. Yes, some of the chapters overlap in terms of time with others, but that's hardly an issue. The forward movement is what really matters. It gives the book its drive, and its destination: the defeat of the first major pandemic of the 21st century.

Then I realized I needed another chapter at the very end that was like the last section of a magazine story — in other words, it looked ahead to the future. In the case of the SARS book, I needed to ask, "What did we learn from this? Could the same kind of pandemic happen again? What are we doing to prevent it?"

As we move through the middle game toward the endgame, then, we need to ask, "What is the overall arc of the book going to look like? What are the big pieces going to look like?"

Imagine that the whole book is going to be a 100,000-piece puzzle, because it has 100,000 words. Eventually you're going to have to put all those words in their places to make the whole thing fit. But it doesn't have to be 100,000-piece puzzle at the moment. It needs to be, say, a 20-piece puzzle. So what are those 20 pieces starting to look like?

This helps especially with a novel, where pacing (that is, the amount of information presented in a certain number of words, or of pages) is vital. As a result, if you look at a handful of novels, you may find that they have a fairly consistent length in terms of chapters, which are, say, 6-9 pages long. That seems right to the reader, but the author doesn't want to be trapped into thinking and writing in chunks that are all the same length. Different emotional landscapes demand scenes of different lengths. So if you look more closely at the chapters, many will consist of sections that can vary quite considerably in length, and allow the novelist to create all the different emotional colors we expect in a novel.

(Even so, if you have a good enough reason, break the rules. In William Faulkner's *As I Lay Dying*, there's an entire chapter, spoken in the voice of the boy Vardaman, that consists of one sentence: "My mother is a fish." Bam. That's the whole chapter.)

In narrative non-fiction there's a similar problem, and this came up in the hitchhiking book, *A Hell of A Place to Lose A Cow*. As I wrote it, every chapter was a day's travel. It began with me waking up and it ended with me in a different place going to bed, exhausted. As you can see, that can become monotonous very quickly. My editor suggested bundling days, but that was an arbitrary solution that was likely to cause more problems than it solved. Luckily, I am at heart an essayist, so each chapter became a narrative essay. In other words, it wasn't just a travelogue that recounted everything that happened. Only the important and interesting narrative went into the chapter, which was held together by an insight or series of insights. It was a journey of discovery in an inner sense, as well as an outer one.

Here's another example of structuring, and of the need to keep your mind open and flexible at this midpoint stage. From the very beginning, even before the proposal stage, my book *Guitar: An American Life* had two threads: it was to be a history of the guitar in America, interwoven with the step-by-step story of master luthier Rick Davis making me a custom acoustic guitar.

This, by the way, is a great illustration of my theory that you want every book to enable you to fire on all the cylinders of your personality. I set it up so I was exercising the research/objective side that would enable me to exercise my curiosity and work as a journalist, but I could also exercise the essayist/observer/poetic side, by writing about experience: what was happening around me, how it struck me, what it made me think.

Even so, I found myself gathering bits and pieces of content that didn't fit into either thread, just as the experience with my own asthma didn't fit into the overall structure I had planned for the book, and became the Patient Progress Reports.

Some of them were guitarists' jokes, which were just too good to be left out. In the end I created a Glossary, which is normally a very sober collection of information, but in this case I subverted it and used it as an excuse to gather a variety of humorous tidbits. It turned out to be one of my favorite parts of the book, and many readers felt the same.

Others were incidents or stories that spoke directly to the questions at the heart of the book: What makes the relationship between the guitarist and the guitar, and the guitar and the listener, so special? How does that relationship contribute to the fact that it's the most popular instrument in the country, and outsells all other instruments combined?

When these incidents didn't fit into either thread, I found myself thinking of them as interludes. In the end, I wanted to keep half a dozen of them. My editor, who was very astute, said, "We should keep them." She had them set in a different typeface. She honored that structural imperative, and helped to insure that everything important found its place.

I want to underline that. The purpose of a structure is to make sure that everything important has its place, and that place demonstrates and enhances its importance. It's up to you to decide what is important, and how to show it off to best advantage. You probably want to start thinking about that right now.

NEARLY THERE

THE END OF THE TUNNEL

According to common mythology, the hardest part of writing a book is the beginning. In many ways, though, finishing a book — especially finishing it well — can be just as hard.

As you get close to ending work on a book, your entire sense of what you're trying to achieve has to change. The best way to explain what I mean is to choose an example from outside the world of writing. The Endangered Alphabets project gets me invited to a number of really high-end woodworking shows. These are ones where, say, a nice little dresser, handmade, hand-stained, costs around $6,000.

There's a lot of skill in being able to choose the wood, cut it accurately, dovetail the joints and put all the sliders in so that the drawers actually work, and so on, but the final part matters as much as any of them.

If you go into a woodworker's shop, there's a good chance you'll see the cabinetmaker there with either a polisher, or perhaps a piece of steel wool and some rub-on polyurethane, and what looks like a finished piece of furniture. The cabinetmaker is going over and over this apparently finished piece because he or she knows from bitter experience that you can make a $6,000 dresser and do one sloppy thing at the end, after the thousands of things you've done well, and nobody will buy your work. You've just wasted all that time, all that effort, all that skill, and one hasty/lazy/unconsidered step has cost you $6,000.

As a writer, when you've got to the point where you've pretty much said everything that you want to say and it's pretty much in the right order and you have a sense of the work as a whole, you then have to go from: "What do I want this to be about? How do I want it to be brilliant or sound clever?" to "How can I make this the best book it can possibly be?" And that's the subtle but significant shift from writing to editing.

The human impulse, of course, wants you to do exactly the opposite. Once you've put that much work into it, you don't want to put any more work into it than you have to. So if someone says to you, "Oh, you should do this or you should do that, or you shouldn't have that or you should have more of that," your first reaction is going to be to say, "I don't want to do that. I've been working on this thing now for two years. It's good enough."

Hah!

What may not yet be clear to you is how complex a structure a book really is. It's something like building a boat for the first time. Unless you're an extraordinarily conscientious woodworker, what's going to happen is that you're going to think the boat is finished — looks good, all the pieces seem to be in the right places — but when you put it in the water, it's going to leak from a dozen places. A hundred places. It's going to go down like a lead parrot.

We're not just talking about individual words, or individual sentences. We're talking about ideas, logic, consistency, whether the entire thing holds together.

In fiction, the process of putting the thing in the water can be devastating. I have a novelist friend who submitted a "finished" novel to his editor, who read it and said, essentially, "Meh. You know, I don't like this character. Let's take this character out. And I think we need to have another character here."

In other words, he had to rewrite almost every chapter to some degree, and he had to invent not only a new character but also whole new loops for the plot. He had to rethink, if not rewrite, every single page.

Non-fiction, too, is based on an argument, a sequence of ideas and information that build on each other. If you've made an incorrect assumption or you've forgotten to take a viewpoint into consideration, it could easily torpedo a whole chapter, perhaps more.

At this point, it's hard to see this kind of error by yourself. In a way, your mistakes are a part of yourself, and vice versa; they are embedded in the way you think. What's worse, the mistakes you can spot — the typos, the misspellings — are the most superficial. Fixing them simply misleads you into thinking that your manuscript is now perfect.

In short, then, you've got to bring in the cavalry. You've got to send the manuscript out to people who know what they're talking about (including experts in the field who know more than you do), who care enough about you and your work to want to be as tough on it as they possibly can.

That takes enormous amounts of courage on your part. Especially you're writing a memoir. You may have to check in with family members. You've got to say to them, "Here's what I've written. I realize you may see things differently, or remember things differently. Please let me know if you think I've forgotten something, or misunderstood something, especially if it's something you said or did. In the end we may not see everything exactly the same way, but I don't want to get anything flat-out wrong, and I don't want to hurt anyone's feelings."

(Of course, if you're writing an expose and you actually do want to hurt someone's feelings, you don't send the manuscript to them. You send it to a lawyer.)

Members of your book group or writing group, I'm sorry to say, are not necessarily good readers for your nearly finished manuscript. There can be a lot of internal politics within these groups, and a certain element of competition. Plus, you want to support each other, but at this point you don't need support — you need rigor. It's probably better to get a reader who is hard-nosed outsider.

Here's what can happen if you don't go through this humbling process. When I wrote *Thirty Percent Chance of Enlightenment*, I was feeling enormously grateful to a couple in southern India who bailed me out of trouble, gave me all kinds of help and insights, and were pretty much the heroes of the book. I sent them a copy of the manuscript, and they asked me to remove a sentence that unintentionally insulted them, purely because of cultural ignorance on my part. I thought I understood the mistake and changed the offending sentence, instead of removing it — and then didn't send it back to them for confirmation. In fact, I had misunderstood their objection, and the correction was worthless.

When the book was printed I sent a substantial package of copies to them to send to all their friends and family. The cost of books plus shipping was over $300. When they read the book, they were aghast. "What have we done," they demanded, "to make you want to hurt us like this?"

I had no option. I apologized, feeling terrible, made the correction, and swallowed the $300, which I could ill afford. The fact is, no full-time professional editor would have caught that mistake. There was no protecting me from the consequences of my writing other than to make sure before I went to print that I knew what I was doing.

That's also why I have come to respect those demonic voices in your head that every so often say, "How could you make this elementary error and not include this piece of information?" "Who do you think you are to actually be writing a book on this subject?" They are not to be taken so seriously that you give up writing, but they are useful reminders that you are, indeed, going to print, that people will take what you publish seriously, and you had damn well better know what you're talking about.

I FOUGHT THE LAW

Let's start out by stating the obvious: I am not a lawyer. I am not in any way qualified to give legal advice, and if you believe a word I say you have nobody to blame but yourself. That being said, I offer you the usual warnings offered by writers to other writers in this situation.

The legal questions I hear from first-time authors fall on both sides of the legal fence — basically, who might sue me, and who might I have to sue?

The second question is a little easier, though both have to be prefaced with the usual warning that if in doubt, pony up and pay the lawyer, even if only for peace of mind.

The second question is generally expressed as "How do I know nobody's going to steal my work?"

This is a much greater cause of anxiety now that so much writing appears in digital form — in emails, on websites, in eBooks. Digital copying and pasting is not only far, far easier than sitting in front of an open book and laboriously typing it out — it's also such an ingrained habit that even people who are ardent supporters of copyright protection find themselves sending their friends YouTube clips, photos, articles, and all the other intellectual roadkill of the digital age.

Yet theft is unlikely to be much of a problem for you. By and large, outright theft (as opposed to casual borrowing) happens only when there's a significant sum of money involved. You may have that problem one day, and I hope you do, but for now I doubt anyone is going to steal your entire manuscript and claim it as his or her own. The time and effort simply don't justify the risk.

In fact, to turn the question around, you may well want to offer part or parts of your book up to the digital vultures. Long before you finish your manuscript you should already have set up a website for your book, and you would do well to offer teasing little snippets at regular intervals, either on your site, or on your blog, or on Twitter, or through whatever other social media you prefer.

These could be pithy little truths, especially if you're writing non-fiction/self-help/advice. An Insight of the Week feature may well help to grow your readers' sense of anticipation, and if people retweet/republish/forward your little nuggets, so much the better. And you will of course have set up a PayPal button on your site so people can pre-order your book.

I have offered a downloadable pdf for one of my books as a teaser, and on another occasion published an entire book in episodes. Both turned out to be successful strategies, especially the second, and I've never heard of anyone copying all the episodes, patching them together, and republishing them as his or her own work. The theft issue, then, is likely to be much more of a threat for music and movies than books, at least for the time being.

Now let's shift over to the other side of the fence and consider whether anyone is likely to sue you.

Although there are guidelines for what an author may or may not say in print, the sad fact (as explained to me by a lawyer) is that anyone can sue you for any reason, if they feel like it.

The best illustration I've seen of this threat, or to be more precise of the fear of this threat, was a Random House attorney's letter concerning my book *Signs of Life*. The cover letter indicated that the attorney had read the manuscript and saw nothing actionable in it; but he then appended five pages, single-spaced, of words, phrases or sentences that might be edited or amended to reduce the threat of litigation from none to less than none, presumably. I ignored most of the recommendations, but frankly if my editor had been of a more anxious cast of mind, she might have insisted on my rewriting every last one.

In this mess of legal uncertainty, I'm going to suggest you apply the Writing Karma principle.

Writing has many kinds of appeal to the writer, but one of the most powerful and seductive is that *it is your writing*. You're no longer in tenth grade; nobody is going to whack your knuckles with a ruler if you use the first person pronoun. Or to make a less juvenile point: writing is like a dream. It allows you to roam the vast gardens of your imagination and spend your time in the company of people you are free to love and hate and clothe and converse with entirely as you please.

Under these sublime conditions, it is very, very easy to write as though you are, indeed, dreaming, and what you say will have no impact outside your own skull. In fact, even if you have quite a clear awareness of your reader and how you want him or her to react to your book, you may at the same time have casually sideswiped a couple of people here and there who, you feel, totally deserved it.

You may even have the sense that you're sitting there chuckling and rubbing your hands together at the prospect of justice finally being served, thanks to your wit. Trust me, I've been there too.

This is not only dangerous, but cowardly. Writing is a form of conversation at which only one side is present at the moment. My suggestion, after thirty years of writing in the public realm, is to write only what you would say to someone's face.

Sure, there are exceptions. If you're writing about the genocidal actions of a military dictator, you may want to violate this rule from a safe distance. But in general, your book will give you the equivalent of a fairly large baseball bat, and a sentence in chapter twelve may well wield more power than you do in real-life conversation. In fact, that's exactly why you may succumb to the temptation to trash someone in writing. But the very person who may ignore your comments in real life may decide to sue the person who is wielding that huge baseball bat in print.

In my non-lawyerly experience, readers of a generally moderate temperament think of suing under two circumstances: if they feel abused, and/or if they feel there may be a sizeable chunk of money to be unearthed.

If you have deep pockets, or even if you look as thought you may have deep pockets, or if you're even employed by someone who looks as though they may have deep pockets, you're more likely to be at risk of litigation. And under those circumstances, it's pretty hard to predict who may sue you, or why.

In general, then, you want to avoid making people feel attacked. That doesn't necessarily mean you have to water down everything you write; it means you have to remember that a book is like one side of a conversation. In other words, you may want to do the very last thing you feel like doing: talking to the person you may be offending before you go to print.

This may sound as though you're walking into a firefight, and indeed that may happen. But if you alert the person and offer him or her a chance to present his or her point of view before you go to print, you stand a chance of defusing the crisis a little, and it's even possible you may decide you were hasty, and want to revise your opinion somewhat.

It may seem to you, the author, that it is the unreasonable person who sues — but in truth it's often the unreasonable person who is sued.

WHY YOU NEED AN EDITOR

(OR AT LEAST A REASONABLE FACSIMILE THEREOF)

If you have enough courage and belief in yourself to write a book, you might also believe that you are a strong writer and have no need of an editor. You couldn't be more wrong.

To get you to see what I mean, let's start with the assumption that you want this to be the best book you can write on this particular subject. (If you don't have that ambition, you actually don't need an editor. But if that level of mediocrity is your goal, you're probably not reading this book.)

So let's address a question you may not have considered: how do you make sure you have got the very best of your thinking onto the page?

It's not a bad idea to start at the very end of the writing/editing process and move backwards, because that sequence helps move us from the familiar to the less familiar.

The last stage of the writing/editing process is proofreading. In theory, this is a process that doesn't address the thinking that you, the author, have put into the book. It assumes that all your mental ducks are in a series of rows, or flocks, or some other useful pattern, and the proof-reader simply spots typos or misplaced quotation marks or other slips of the finger that need to be corrected.

In truth, a good proofreader does more than that. Even at this very late stage he or she may notice that, for example, you have used the word "basically" or the phrase "for example" seven times per page, and will suggest you vary your reader's diet. Already this apparently small-potato intervention is starting to illustrate how poorly we, as writers, are equipped to observe and organize our own thinking.

I chose those examples because even though I'm a very organized thinker, words such as "basically" and phrases such as "for example" are parts of the verbal process I use to organize my thought. I'm probably the last person to notice myself overusing them. This is exactly the point for this chapter, in fact. Writing isn't just like taking Scrabble tiles out of your mind and laying them on the board of your page. It's an extraordinarily complex and dynamic process that even as it takes places tends to change who we are, what we're thinking, what we want to say, and how we translate that desire into words. And while we're in the middle of that electrical brainstorm, we're very poorly equipped to step outside ourselves and see our writing from our reader's point of view, even at the level of typos and punctuation. Looking inward, our eyes glaze over. We see so much inner life we miss much of the outer life we're creating. We need help.

The next step backwards is the copyediting phase.

Inexperienced writers tend to have two misconceptions about copyediting. One is that it is the same as proofreading, and as such just involves a kind of verbal cleanup, a light shave and a haircut.

The other is that copyediting is what is really meant by editing — namely, that all editing just involves a kind of verbal cleanup, a light shave and a haircut.

Let's deal with the first of these misconceptions first. Copyediting certainly aims to produce consistency, and often consistency to the principles of a style manual. But mistakes are mistakes for a reason. Grammar is the science of clarity. If you've made a grammar mistake, or misused a word or a piece of punctuation, it's not just that a cosmic seventh-grade teacher is going to look down from some chalky Heaven and deduct points from your likelihood of enjoying a comfortable afterlife. If you've made a grammar mistake, you've made your work harder for your reader to understand — and, after all, you want your reader to understand what you're trying to say. Even corrections of syntax, punctuation, spelling, diction, and grammar, then, are clarifications of your thinking.

But a good copy-editor clarifies in many other ways. A sentence may be clearer if you reverse some of the word order. A paragraph may be clearer if split into two, or rearranged. All of these operations are not simply tinkering with your text; they are interventions into the wiring of your thought. And as such, a skilled outside observer will see things you flat-out miss — confusing tangles of verbiage you've read over time and again without seeing that they are, in fact, bad writing. Or even just dull, abstract, or dry writing that could be much juicier, more vivid, more powerful.

Nobody's attention is consistently at its sharpest. Everyone gives more thought here than there. For every spot-on phrase, another comes along that is tired, clichéd, inexact, flabby, or just wrong. Remember how I said at the start of this chapter, "Let's start with the assumption that you want this to be the best book you can write on this particular subject"? That means you want your attention to be at its sharpest for every single word. You may need help to sustain that degree of rigor.

The person who should, in theory, scour your manuscript before it goes to the copy-editor is a fact-checker. It's a sad truth that very few publishing operations employ fact-checkers any more, relying (ha!) on the author to check his or her facts. A good copy-editor may well take on some or all of the duties of a fact-checker. I've benefited from some wonderful copy-editors, one of whom spent hours trying to discern whether the guitarist in the Count Basie Orchestra spelled his name Green or Greene. But that degree of conscientiousness is not a given. It's also not a given in you, the author. I can promise you, by the time you're this close to the end of the book-writing process, the temptation to shrug and say, "ah, close enough" is going to be almost overwhelming.

You'd do well to address the issue of fact-checking in one (or both) of two ways.

You can bribe a friend or hire a bright student to do it for you. Fact-checking is not, in fact, all that hard; it just takes diligence and a certain resourcefulness, and it's a lot easier if you can tell your fact-checker what sources you used for your information so he or she can retrace your steps.

On the other hand, you can send your manuscript out to one or (preferably) more experts in the field who really know your subject well, possibly people you have met and befriended along the way.

And don't imagine this reaching-out is a sign of weakness. Pick up any book by your favorite author and look at the Acknowledgments page. See that lengthy list of names? Most of those were involved in research and/or fact checking. Go, and do thou likewise.

Now we're finally getting back toward the beginning of the editing phase, but even here editing takes place at various levels. The last stage is line editing, which works on the common-sense level of "Does this sentence make sense? Is it exactly what you meant?" But this issue of "what you meant" is far subtler than it seems, and goes to the heart of this chapter.

Perhaps the best way to illustrate what editing is all about is to use an analogy. Imagine a stranger with an impressive-looking over-the-shoulder digital video camera comes up to you on the street and asks, "What is the most valuable and important thing you've learned in your life?"

Fiction writers, consider a different question: "What is the most interesting, complex, profound story you know?"

Sheesh, you think. *Give me a moment…*

It's not that you haven't learned anything important or valuable in your life, or you haven't heard any fascinating stories — it's that you may not have put them together clearly and coherently into words so this dude's viewers will be able to grasp what you mean.

You quickly sort through all the various life discoveries you've made or stories you've heard, but even when you've picked one, you have to figure out where to start, what to include, how to make the drama and importance of the subject clear.

It's a next-to-impossible task. (This is why good reporters ask focused, specific questions, in fact, as they're much easier to answer.) It would be easier if you had someone ask you intelligent, perceptive, directing questions that helped you feel through the tangles of barely-worded thought in your mind; it would be easier if you had someone lead you from one step to the next; it would be easier if someone asked you to try explaining yourself in different words every time they didn't quite follow your drift.

This is the weakness of writing. If we wipe out the reporter and replace him with your best friend, and we take you off the street and place the two of you at your kitchen table, then you would have a far better chance of making yourself understood. Your friend is there nodding, or looking puzzled, or asking you all kinds of questions that help you organize your criss-crossing trains of thought, and with this constant feedback you may muddle your way through to the grand, overarching point you're trying to make.

A writer, especially a solitary writer, doesn't have that luxury. Every sentence you write implies multiple questions (*Really? Why? What were you thinking? Who's that? What happened next?*), and you're left trying to anticipate what they are. Writing is only one side of a dialogue, but it has to anticipate the other side. It's like a scientific experiment involving a conversation between two people separated not by a pane of clear glass but by a mirror. You have to guess what the person behind the glass is thinking, how they're reacting. And that's where your editor comes in.

Your editor is, at various levels, the reporter asking the big question, your best friend eliciting your big idea, and the scientific researcher informing you sentence by sentence how your remote listener is reacting to what you're saying.

Once you understand all those roles, you may be lucky enough to have a friend or friends you can enlist to help you with each of them, though they need to be literate, dedicated, inquisitive, crisp in thought, compassionate, firm, articulate, and organized.

Failing that, you may need to hire an editor.

Hiring a professional editor is harder than hiring a plumber. More people use plumbers, so it's easier to get recommendations. Moreover, most trades require some kind of certification, whereas editors are a far more free-ranging bunch. Worst of all, there's no trade school for editors — in fact, there's no school at all. Good luck finding someone with a degree in book editing — in fact, good luck finding a degree program that includes even a single course in book editing. Editors learn on the job, and not even a good writer is necessarily a good editor.

Your best and only bet is to ask to see samples of the editor's work, in the area or genre in which you yourself are writing. Don't judge it by the status of the client or the quality of the printing — look at the writing. A good editor is like a safety net: no matter how ragged the writing, the editor raises it to an acceptable standard of professionalism. Are the samples clear, interesting, potent? If so, that's the editor you want. If they're not, don't accept excuses.

Please don't think I'm talking down to you. I'm not saying you need help because you're a beginner — though I'm certainly saying that, as a beginner, you definitely need help. But the fact is, we all need help.

Here's the kind of thing I mean. It may look to you as though I wrote this book, or indeed all of my books. And bear in mind that I'm an experienced writer, editor and writing teacher, and my editors regularly praise me for my clean copy — that is, the writing I send them needs relatively little editing. But here's what happened.

I realized four years ago I should probably pull together some of these thoughts for the first-time book writers who were approaching the Champlain College Publishing Initiative. I jotted down maybe 20 pages of notes and veered off into other projects.

A little less than a year ago I came back to the topic and

dictated another twenty pages of notes that were transcribed by two amazing students, Molly Abrahamson and Taylor Covington. My friend and colleague Kim MacQueen, a writer, teacher, and gifted editor, read over the "manuscript" (in truth a messy pile of sections and paragraphs, full of redundancies and gaps), identified the most important topics that struck her as missing or incomplete, and asked me a series of questions to address those holes.

More transcription followed, and the messy pile came back to me. I reorganized most of the sections, added a dozen new chapters, rewrote most of the dictated material (which was full of all kinds of colloquial inexactitudes), added a great deal of explanation and some nifty turns of phrase, and passed it back to Kim.

In a sense, then, a great deal of large-scale editing had already taken place. What Kim did next, using Track Changes in Microsoft Word, consisted of edits on what might be thought of as the micro scale and the macro scale. She made 135 micro edits (fixes of typos, punctuation, capitalization, spacing, formatting, and so on) and 43 macro edits. The macro edits, which she usually posed as suggestions, comments, or questions, suggested cuts, clarifications, amplifications, requests for new information, suggestions that sentences, paragraphs or entire chapters be moved to a more suitable location. She also pointed out that I used one analogy not twice but *four times*. So much for that Oxford education, eh?

Of course, we're by no means done. I'm working on those edits — which include this entire chapter, which was her idea — but the resulting draft will go back to her again, not just once but several times, I expect. That's what's called writing. That's what we do.

EDIT, DON'T TINKER

If you can't afford a professional editor and you don't have well-qualified friends, you can do what we all do at some point, and try to edit your own work. It's not ideal, and it's not easy, but it may be the best you can manage. Given that, I have a few suggestions.

In the late Eighties I got an assignment for the *Atlantic Monthly* to write an article about the new National Curriculum that was being introduced in the United Kingdom.

At that time it was the highest-profile assignment I'd landed, and I was very aware of what good it might do my writing career. They were also going to pay me the biggest fee I'd ever had, and they were going to fly me to England so I could do the reporting. On top of that, education is a subject that interests me a great deal, and I knew I could do as good a job as anyone on this story.

I flew to England, I gathered vast amounts of information, I conducted interviews — I was in good shape. I came back, gathered my thoughts, and began writing the 4,500-5,500 words. I wrote a draft, went back in and rewrote it, went back in and rewrote it again. By then I was an experienced journalist; I knew what I was doing.

Yet a strange thing began to happen. As friends heard about

the assignment and asked me about it, I found myself ducking or deflecting their questions. It was bizarre: the pinnacle of my writing career to date, yet I was avoiding talking about it.

Eventually it hit me. I was afraid that if I started talking about the subject, they'd be bored. Which meant that even though I hadn't admitted it to myself, I was bored.

There was only one thing to do. I had to stop tinkering with the story and start the whole thing from scratch, writing it as if I were telling a stranger what was going on in education in the U.K., and why it was important.

I changed probably the entire first quarter of the story, and reframed almost everything else. The tone changed, the diction changed, the argument changed. Only then did I send it to the editor, and it ran about a year later.

Here's the point: we all like to believe we can nail it first time. Whatever it is: journalism, fiction, memoir, how-to. We like to think that even if we haven't nailed every single word, we've pretty much got it down on paper, and all it needs now is just a shave and a haircut.

Wrongggg!

As soon as we make that false assumption, we start down a very, very wrong path. We start to tinker. We play with a word or two here and there instead of looking at the thing as a whole. At best, we copy-edit when we should be editing.

While we're at it, let's make a clear distinction between editing and copyediting. Editing is the process by which the manuscript becomes the most powerful, effective, memorable piece of writing it can possibly be. Copyediting is the process of making that text clean, consistent and grammatically accurate. Both are important, but the point I want to make as forcefully as I can is that you're not ready for copyediting yet. You haven't yet made it the best piece of writing it can be.

What makes this tough is that you haven't got an editor working on your behalf to wrestle the text into shape. You've got to do it yourself at a time when, as my friend, fellow-teacher and fellow-editor Larry Connolly puts it, you are blind. You've been working on your manuscript so long you just can't see the whole sprawling forest for the lines of trees. Frankly, it may well be worth hiring an editor. But if you're determined to go it alone, consider four questions, each of which, handily, involves the letter C.

IS IT CLEAR?

Ideas, words, phrases, trains of thought that are familiar to you — because they're yours! — may not be at all clear to your reader. If in doubt, you want to simplify and clarify. Yes, there are occasions when writers want to be deliberately ambiguous, or to hold information back to create suspense, but in general, as a first-time author, you want to err on the side of clarity over cleverness. When someone says to you, "I really liked that story/poem/essay," but when it comes down to it, they can't really say or remember what it was about, you realize it's time to clean up your writing.

You want to challenge yourself to be as clear as possible at every level of detail. On the largest scale: does the overall organization of the book (the plot, the argument, the train of thought) make sense? Is the same true at the chapter level? Is each paragraph crisp, with a strong beginning and end, or does it try to make too many points and as a result muddy them all together? Is each sentence like a crisp musical phrase, or have you lapsed into trying to impress the reader? Are you, in fact, thinking of your reader, and how you're trying to affect him or her, *all the time?*

It's no exaggeration that when I look over anything I write, without exception, I find ways to make it clearer, stronger, punchier.

IS IT CREDIBLE?

This question means slightly different things under different circumstances.

In non-fiction, especially non-fiction based on reporting or research, it means, "Have you accumulated the facts that support your thesis, or your conclusions?" If not, your entire book could be in danger of falling apart.

In fiction, it may mean, "Would person A really act like that?" It may mean something more fundamental, though — namely, "Do you know what you're talking about?" For your fiction to be credible, you can't rely simply on your imagination. You've got to do the homework. And that means not only editing but researching and editing. Sorry. No choice.

IS IT COMPLETE?

This is the hardest part of editing, because it is much, much more difficult to see what is *not* there than what is.

Lack of completeness springs from the simple fact that *the reader does not know what you know.* This is one of the many valuable lessons of travel writing: the reader has not been where you have been and seen what you have seen, so when you write, say, the word "market," you have a picture in your mind's eye that is teeming with movement, colors, sounds, smells — but your reader has just one word, and even that word probably conjures up an entirely wrong mental image.

Your job as a writer, then, is to leave the reader's mind teeming with everything teeming in your own mind. You may forget to do that; you may actively avoid doing that because you don't want to burden the reader with detail; you may think it's your job to be as swift and concise as you can. Yet if you think of your own experience as a reader, you want your mind to come away teeming.

In part it's a simple matter of comprehension: you have to explain and/or illustrate what you're talking about or the reader will get the wrong idea. But it's also a matter of joy — the joy of recalling all that life and writing it, the joy of sharing those experiences.

Still, it's hard, no doubt, to read over your manuscript and realize what you've left out. This is where a friendly reader can help. My suggestion is to give your ally/friend/roommate/fellow writer your manuscript in small chunks, maybe a chapter, maybe even less, and, when they've read the chunk ask them specifically, "What did you want to know more about?"

At first they'll be hesitant, and they may even not know what you're talking about. When you explain, though, they'll start getting into it, and after a while they'll be giving you more feedback than you want. You'll start thinking you need to rewrite the book, and that the revised version will be 2,000 pages long. But use your common sense. You can't include everything. Be judicious; choose the expansions you think are important, worthwhile, interesting, just plain fun.

And once you've written your book out into all these hitherto missing dimensions, you now need to look in the opposite direction and ask....

IS IT CONCISE?

The "less is more" rule applies to writing far more than we like to believe. When I was writing essays for NPR, I got pretty good at distilling what I wanted to say down toward the two minutes fifteen seconds limit, and every time I emailed my copy to the producer I was convinced I had achieved a masterpiece of brevity and precision. And sometimes I had indeed managed to come in at 2:10 or 2:13. (They had some clever software that could look at a text and gauge how long it would take to read it aloud.)

Probably one time in two, though, my producer would say, "We need to lose five seconds."

Every writer should be in that position for some period in his or her life. It was a very salutary experience. I'd go back into the text, find a couple of words here or there or a whole sentence, and cut down to the limit. But here's the point: in every case, once I'd recorded the thing at its new abbreviated length, *those few words now seemed extraneous.* If I imagined writing them back in, the whole thing seemed just that little bit flabbier, more diluted.

The essay was now so strong you could see every one of its abs. Why put the fat back on?

In point of fact, these last two editing phases tend to alternate for some time, like the aftershocks of an earthquake oscillating between up and down phases. Flesh it out, trim it down, fill out, cut back. You have to have both contradictory skills in your editing repertoire. Did anyone say this was going to be easy?

WRITE HERE, EDIT THERE

The good news is that in certain kinds of books you can actually begin this rigorous finishing phase while you're still writing.

As I've already said, it often helps to write in fragments, chunks, or sections. If you've followed my suggestion in this respect, this editing stage can actually begin at different times for different sections of your book.

Let's say you're writing this thing in four sections. It's very possible that you're having a devil of a job getting in touch with one person who's a crucial source of information, whether it's factual information or they're going to give you insights. Let's say that person is central to section three. Unless what they're going to do is change everything in the whole book, which seems unlikely, you can actually start editing sections one and two while you're waiting for this person to become available. This is not only a time-saver, it's also a very healthy mental exercise, because it means you're not just stuck, unable to do anything while you're waiting.

Secondly, it makes you that much more aware of the different drives that are at work in something as large and complicated as a book. It makes you respect them more. If you've been thinking of that fiery first draft (what the poet Coleridge called "the hot fit of composition") as being somehow more real or more important than the research that preceded it or the editing that follows it, you can now see that they're all essential, as you move back and forth from one phase to another.

Thirdly, I tend to think of the writing brain or the writing soul as being like a battery that consists of a number of different cells. But the cells are hooked up in such a way that one of them can run all the way down, and when that happens, you're not going to get anything else out of it. If, however, you can switch to a different battery cell and continue the work, then the cell that has run down will gradually recharge itself.

I discovered how to harness these energies in a peculiarly effective way when I was writing *A Hell of a Place to Lose a Cow*, my hitchhiking book.

It was one of those fertile subjects that offer almost too many ideas. I couldn't wait to get to work in the morning, and as soon as I sat down I could barely type as fast as the sentences occurred to me. I battered away at the keyboard in my two-fingered fashion until I was exhausted — which turned out to be only about 45 minutes. The hot fit of composition was so all-consuming that I couldn't sustain it for much longer, and if I tried to, I just sat there staring at the screen, drained.

At first this was almost unbearably frustrating. Having too many ideas turned out to be pretty much as tough as having too few. After a while, though, I got up grumpily and acknowledged that as it was now June in Vermont I had better go out and mow the low-level forest we euphemistically called a lawn, which at that time of year reached knee-height in a matter of days.

The lawn was muddy in places, sandy in other places, and bumpy all over. We had a horrible lawnmower with the weight and temperament of a mechanical rhino, so I would stamp away from my high-intensity verbal creation, pull on my boots, go outdoors and wrestle the rhino. As I was struggling to mow the lawn, though, I found myself asking myself different questions about the book, thinking about the structure, or wondering whether a certain section was even going to go into it or not. Those are the kinds of things that you don't need to be actually writing to be working on.

After maybe half an hour I gave up on the lawn, went back indoors, got into the shower to wash all the mud and grass clippings off my legs, and by then my ideas had begun to coalesce into words and phrases and I was ready to write again. Rinse (literally) and repeat. This went on for days. It turned into one of the most productive phases of my writing life.

The other value to working on different sections of your book at different times is that you can focus more consciously and deliberately on the technical aspects of your writing.

Okay, yes, I have a degree from Oxford and I direct a college writing program, but that doesn't mean my text is perfectly clean, and every sentence comes out as pure and gleaming as a stream-washed pebble. I still spell some words the British way. I am addicted to dashes. I hyphenate like crazy. I massively overuse colons. Massively. I've literally gone through an entire book manuscript using the search function and looked at every single colon and have been horrified to discover that I had a paragraph of a dozen lines that had seven colons in it. It's because of the way I think. I make an assertion and then I go on and explain it. That's why the colon was invented. But even so, you can't write like that, because it drives the reader insane.

Even if I've written something correctly, that doesn't mean I've written it well. This text you're reading right now — I have sat for hours, mostly in my favorite coffee shops, trying to make complicated sentences simpler and clearer. I can come up with great ideas that some people don't understand, but there's no virtue to that. I want to come up with great ideas that people understand, that fire their energy and their imagination. Reading first-draft sentences can often be like crawling through thickets of brambles. At this stage, my job is to prune them all back until what's left is shining and strong. Bam. Like that.

KILL THE BASTARD

Even though you may have set out with the ambition to write the best bloody book you possibly could, and even though at every stage of the process you may have lived up to that ambition, the hardest time to maintain that standard is at the end.

All of the fun stuff, the exploratory stuff, the bright new ideas, the initial investigation, the stuff you've turned up that no one else had—you've done all of that. Right now it's the bloody colon. Am I overusing the colon? The only way to survive this period is to have the mentality of that cabinetmaker obsessively buffing that piece of furniture. You've got to be going over every single bloody word in your book, saying to yourself whoever looks at this thing, from whatever angle, the light is just going to shine right off it.

A very useful exercise or activity—and this is a way that you can make use of a willing friend as opposed to an expert reader—is to have someone read it and then explain it back to you. This exercise works for a fundamental law of communication: you can't explain what you don't understand. As an author, it's all too possible that you understand what you're trying to say, but you haven't passed it over to the reader with enough clarity. Better find that out now rather than later. Otherwise you're in the situation I found myself in while revising when I gave someone a copy of *Thirty Percent Chance of Enlightenment* only to have her come back and say, "I like it, but I have to say, I still don't really understand what a monsoon is." Eeek. Too late to change it now. The damage was done.

Here's another exercise: have a friend read the book and then ask them what they remember. Good art is memorable. The stuff that your friends remember, then, is not only clear but important. If you've written something they don't remember, then that's not a good sign.

One last story about the process of finishing your book: it was perfectly clear how I should end my first book, *Catching My Breath*. Fairly early on I identified about a dozen aspects of the subject of asthma that I planned to tackle, and when had them all fairly well nailed down, there was nowhere else to go. My second book, *Signs of Life*, was much harder to end because it was really a narrative essay, and even after the principal events ended I was still making discoveries about life, death and care for the terminally ill. I felt the book would never be finished until I had fully understood and explained the full meaning of life and death, and it was becoming clear that not only would I not become that wise before I hit my deadline, I might not become that wise before I died.

I could have kept on tinkering with it forever. What's more, I was doing a magazine article on hospice right after I finished the book, and I would have had every excuse to set the book aside for a while, do the magazine article, see what I learned in the process, and then distilled that latest phase of learning back into the book. I was starting to drag my feet. I wasn't really in deadline trouble because I always stay ahead of deadline. If that means writing throughout the night, I write throughout the night. I make sure I get the stuff done. But when is done done?

Luckily, right around that time, I met an English writer named John Hall. He was introduced to me as someone who had written, as I recall, eight books. Academic books, rather than the kind of books that I was writing, but even so he had to figure out each time how to know when he was done.

So I went to see John Hall — always take every opportunity to talk to writers who have written more than you, by the way — and asked him, "John, how do you know when you're finished? I've got this book I've been working on for two years, and it could be finished, or I could keep tinkering with this and that for another two years. How do you know when you're done?"

He chuckled, and said, "Tim, sometimes you just have to kill the bastard."

I took him to mean something like, "Tim, this book is important to you now, and it may have been the most important thing in your life over the last couple of years, but at some point you've got to move on. You will write other books. But the only way you'll go on to write those other books is if you kill this one — or, to be a little less brutal, you lay it to rest."

Otherwise, in the end, there's no book at all. Your editor is saying, "You're now six months behind; I'm canceling your contract." Or if you're self-publishing, your friends are saying, "What ever happened to that book you said you were writing?"

Okay. Now I'm now going to give you what appears to be utterly contradictory advice. Too bad. That's life. Here we go.

The quality of your final product has not so much to do with how imaginative a writer you are, how fluently you write, or how substantial your vocabulary — it has to do with *the standard to which you hold yourself.*

The most brilliant writers have their hasty moments, their slapdash efforts, their periods of laziness or distraction. We're all human. Every time I give a reading, looking impressive up there with a critically acclaimed, professionally edited book in my hand, I'm actually thinking, "My God! That sentence has eight S's in it! How the hell did I ever miss that?" Or "That is the clumsiest sentence ever written! I could barely read it out loud!"

This book, for all of your polishing and sanding — it's not going to be perfect. It's got to be as perfect as you can make it, but in a year's time you're going to look back at this and say to yourself, "I could have done that so much better. I could have fixed this or that." You have to accept that paradox. It has to be the best book you can possibly do, and you have to accept that it's not perfect. All you can do at this late stage is to be *as diligent as time and circumstances will allow.*

Think of that cabinetmaker. That's got to be you. No matter what you're writing, no matter who's going to read it, you've got to give them the best you can do. That's why we write, and it's why readers read. To see you at your best.

Would you really want any less?

ACKNOWLEDGMENTS

The subject for this book was suggested by my admirable colleague Warren Baker, and when it was flagging the endeavor was revived by Kim MacQueen, who has acted as supporter and editor in the gentlest way imaginable. Cindy Barnes added her editing acumen, and the amazing Taylor Covington and Molly Abrahamson, future authors and editors both, helped by transcribing the barely intelligible content I dictated into my iPhone while driving to Boston and back.

In a broader sense, though, I've learned from all my editors, my writing students, and all the writers and other clients we have worked with at the Champlain College Publishing Initiative. Watching a succession of first-time authors bringing us their epic endeavors and trying to help them across the finish line has taught me more about writing than I ever learned in college.

To all of you, my respect and thanks.

Champlain College Students Janina Hartley, Abel German, Amanda Schroth, and Jude Dircks provided invaluable help and guidance. Champlain Books Intern Claire MacQueen provided editorial support.

The Champlain College Publishing Initiative (CCPI) was created in order to provide Champlain College students with first-hand experience in the field of publishing. CCPI's mission is to play an active part in the great experiment that is publishing in the twenty-first century.

Burlington, Vermont
March 2014

www.ingramcontent.com/pod-product-compliance
Lightning Source LLC
Chambersburg PA
CBHW071226090426
42736CB00014B/2990